Careers in Mental Health

Careers in Mental Health

Opportunities in Psychology, Counseling, and Social Work

Kim Metz, Ph.D.

WILEY Blackwell

This edition first published 2016
© 2016 John Wiley & Sons, Ltd.

Registered Office
John Wiley & Sons, Ltd, The Atrium, Southern Gate, Chichester, West Sussex, PO19 8SQ, UK

Editorial Offices
350 Main Street, Malden, MA 02148-5020, USA
9600 Garsington Road, Oxford, OX4 2DQ, UK
The Atrium, Southern Gate, Chichester, West Sussex, PO19 8SQ, UK

For details of our global editorial offices, for customer services, and for information about how to apply for permission to reuse the copyright material in this book please see our website at www.wiley.com/wiley-blackwell.

The right of Kim Metz to be identified as the author of this work has been asserted in accordance with the UK Copyright, Designs and Patents Act 1988.

Library of Congress Cataloging-in-Publication Data

Names: Metz, Kim, author.
Title: Careers in mental health : opportunities in psychology, counseling,
   and social work / Kim Metz, Ph.D.
Description: Chichester, West Sussex ; Malden, MA : John Wiley & Sons, Inc.,
   2016. | Includes bibliographical references and index.
Identifiers: LCCN 2015040818 (print) | LCCN 2015043939 (ebook) |
   ISBN 9781118767924 (pbk.) | ISBN 9781119221111 (pdf) | ISBN 9781118768440 (epub)
Subjects: LCSH: Mental health services–Vocational guidance.
Classification: LCC RA790.75 .M48 2016 (print) | LCC RA790.75 (ebook) |
   DDC 362.2023–dc23
LC record available at http://lccn.loc.gov/2015040818

A catalogue record for this book is available from the British Library.

Cover image: Getty/Martin Spurny

Set in 10.5/13.5pt Galliard by SPi Global, Pondicherry, India

Printed and bound in Malaysia by Vivar Printing Sdn Bhd

1   2016

Contents

Acknowledgments

I first and foremost want to acknowledge all of the students whom I have taught and advised over the years. They were the true inspiration for writing this text. I sincerely care that they make good life choices and I was distressed that they didn't have a place to review all of the options in mental health careers easily. Additionally, I have had other professors tell me that they have the same struggle with their own students, and they urged me to put pen to paper so that they could use the information with their own students/advisees. So, thank you also to my colleagues, the ones in my department at Walsh University and the ones with whom I have met and conversed at conferences, for their encouragement.

Second, I'd like to thank Walsh University for granting me a sabbatical in order to get started with this textbook. Time away in an endeavor different from your usual duties is stimulating, and this work would have been impossible without the uninterrupted time; it also invigorated me when I returned to my students the following semester.

Finally, I have to thank my family for giving me many, many short sabbaticals while I strived to finish this text after returning to work full time. The patience and support and encouragement of my husband, Kenny, and my two children, Melissa and Jared, was invaluable and so appreciated. I finished, guys!

Introduction

Advisor: Hello, Jane Student. I see that you have your next semester's classes all chosen and you seem to be on track with all of your requirements. Let's talk about what I think is the more important part of advising. What exactly do you want to do with your degree in psychology (or counseling or social work)?
Jane Student: (smiling dreamily) I really want to help people.

After, "I've been closed out of a class" (and I can't write a book to fix THAT problem), the preceding is probably the most common dialogue I have with my advisees. Now, please don't think I'm mocking the exchange. I had the same one with my advisor when I was Jane Student. I begin with this conversation because it was the inspiration for writing this book. You see, I would typically struggle with what my next line in the conversation should be, as there are myriad ways to proceed in order to develop a career helping people with mental health issues.

First, full disclosure – I have a Ph.D. in clinical psychology. Over the last 20 years I have worked in various positions as a psychologist. During my internship I worked in a forensic unit in a prison, in a VA hospital, in an outpatient clinic, and on an adolescent ward of an inpatient hospital. After internship I was the staff psychologist at a juvenile justice facility and later at an adolescent group home. When I began having children of my own, I cut back my work hours and did clinical work part time at a community mental health agency and started teaching part time at a local college. I also achieved the Holy Grail of "helping people" and was an independent contractor at a private practice. I teach full time in a psychology department at a small liberal arts college and continue carrying a small client caseload at a private practice. I can say that I truly enjoyed all of these job opportunities and that I'm confident that I have been able to achieve my goal "helping people" many times over.

OK – back to what to say to Jane Student. Given my background, my first inclination when I began teaching (and advising) full time was to say "great, let's get going on those applications for a Ph.D. clinical psychology graduate program." I would also hand them a copy of one of the many "So You Want to be a Psychology Major" books I always have on my shelf. I'm also not mocking those books. They are very useful, and I referred to one when I was Jane Student as well. However, I quickly found that the books, as well as the Ph.D. in clinical psychology programs, were not appropriate for many of my students.

For example, some students, for family or financial reasons, did not envision at least four more years of school (plus a year-long internship) following college. Others had desire and time, but lacked the grades or the research experience it would take to get into what are very competitive clinical psychology graduate schools. Still others were dead set on not moving more than a few miles away from home, so their pickings of graduate programs in clinical psychology would be slim, to say the least.

Therefore, I wanted to find a more appropriate "next line" in my dialogue with my students. I began to do some research on the various degrees available to assist them in their quest to "help people" and in answer to some of their questions:

- What is the difference between a clinical and counseling psychologist?
- Is a Psy.D. a more appropriate degree than a Ph.D.?
- Mental health counseling? Is that different from what a counseling psychologist does?
- I think I want to do marriage counseling; should I just get a degree in marriage and family therapy?
- Does a social worker make more or less money than a counselor?
- What if I want to work in the schools? What does a school counselor do?
- What types of clients does a social worker help? Are they different from those that a psychologist helps?

I had hoped that I could just find a book on the topic and offer it to them. However, it appeared that any title on the subject dealt only with one type of degree. So, to examine all the alternatives, one would need to read through several books and try to synthesize the information. While I'm certainly not against students needing to synthesize information, I really thought there had to be a more suc-cinct way to educate them about the various opportunities out there. Moreover, it is often difficult for students to get good "reads" on these things because each profession has a strong identity and strongly adheres to its own tenets. Therefore, when asked, many professors and/or professionals may be biased in favor of their own training. Further, many psychology professors who do not have a clinical or counseling background (such as social psychologists, cognitive psy-chologists, or experimental psychologists) are also in the dark about the various paths that students who desire a career in mental health can take. Their careers are more focused on research, and details of the clinical side of the profession are often not at their fingertips. This text can be helpful to those professors as well, since the majority of them will have advising responsibilities for psychology students who hope to "help people" by engaging in some type of counseling or therapy.

My goal is to delineate the similarities and differences in these helping professions in a nonbiased way. To make it easier to compare apples to apples, I have divided each chapter into the same sections:

- Overall philosophy and history of the profession (note that much of the history of the professions is intertwined. I have a section in each chapter for each profession but there may be some overlap.)
- Type of education needed
- The role that licensing plays in your chosen profession
- The types of jobs for which the degree will qualify you
- Earning potential

In this way, students can compare and contrast the various opportu-nities and decide which is right for them. This is an important endeavor because students spend several years in graduate work and are tied to the profession/license they achieve. It is in their best interest to under-stand thoroughly the field in which they are going to practice so that they can make the best decisions for themselves.

Now, having said that, let me make one significant notation. The general public (e.g., you right now) really has very little understanding of the distinctions between these professions. Indeed, the professionals in each discipline often do not understand the differences themselves. Further, the jobs that are available for each profession are often similar. Therefore, the choice you make as to which degree to obtain may not make as big a difference as you might expect. However, my experience with students is that they want to be informed and make choices about their careers, not just rely on some flip of a coin as to which direction they will chart a path.

One more caveat to the information we will be discussing is that I can really only give you a general overview of the information. You will have to take into consideration the specifics of each profession based on the state in which your reside and/or hope to practice. An example of this will be the information on licensing standards and salary, which will vary from state to state.

In the first part of the book I will examine each of the various professions you might choose. I will begin with psychology and discuss doctoral degrees in psychology; that is, Ph.D.s and Psy.D.s in both clinical and counseling psychology. Specifically, the distinctions and differences between these career paths will be discussed. Please understand that there are other specialties in which one can choose to earn a Ph.D. in psychology, such as industrial organizational, experimental, and social. While these specialties no doubt help people, it is typically not in the way that most undergraduates mean when they indicate an interest in helping people. If one of these might be your area of interest, please check out some other titles on graduate work in psychology, as there are several texts available. Next, a discussion of the social work profession and the various career options that exist within it will follow. Then the various types of counseling, including mental health counseling and marriage and, family therapy, will be examined. The specialty of substance abuse follows. Finally, a discussion of mental health professionals who work within the schools, school psychologists and school counselors, will follow.

Readers should also understand that there are career options for students who do not wish to attend graduate school. However, those options won't be covered in this work. One can easily find other manuals written with the "undergraduate degree only" student in mind.

Finally, I will not be discussing psychiatry in this text. As you may know, many people confuse the professions of psychiatry and psychology. Both carry the title of "doctor," but a psychiatrist is an M.D. and a psychologist is a Ph.D. A psychiatrist trains in the same way that every other M.D. trains, that is, 2 years of medical school, 2 years of supervised experience, and 4 years of residency. Psychiatrists will begin their training in the same way, with the same coursework and supervised experience as a pediatrician or a surgeon or an oncologist. It is during their residency that they specialize in their chosen area. For example, if someone chooses to be a psychiatrist, the American Psychiatric Association requires that, after their first year of general medical residency, they must complete 36 months of required psychiatric training. They learn about topics such as psychopathology, psychopharmacology, cognitive behavioral therapy, and substance abuse disorders. Obviously, because of this medical training a psychiatrist can prescribe medication. The psychologist, who attends graduate school instead of medical school, cannot prescribe medication. There is a movement to allow psychologists to gain extra training that could allow them to prescribe psychotropic medication but, in the majority of states, this is still not an option. See Unit 2 for more information about psychologists who are trying to obtain prescription privileges.

The second section of the book will focus on information about what it takes to be effective in the helping professions regardless of which degree or license the student eventually earns. Topics in this section will include matters such matters as:

- Good and bad motivations for choosing a career in the helping professions (e.g., are you hoping to solve others' problems or your own?). This section will include qualities and characteristics that make a good therapist.
- An ethics primer in which basic ethical principles are discussed as well as the impact they have on the helper and the helpee. The ethical principles relating to confidentiality, maintaining boundaries, and record-keeping will be discussed.
- The importance of being a critical thinker and understanding the clinical research so that, no matter which profession you choose, you will be able to discern the most up-to-date and empirically supportive treatments. The useful of this critical thinking in your "real life" will also be explored.

- A discussion of what to do to increase your chances of getting into graduate school. This section will cover how items such as grades, test scores, research experience, letters of recommendation, vitas, a personal statement, interviews, and volunteer or internship opportunities will impact your graduate school application.
- An overview of some of the things that will need to be considered after graduate school and licensing is complete and you are practicing in the field. This chapter will include short sections on continuing education, malpractice insurance, doing therapy using technology, and the possibility of one mental health profession receiving prescription privileges and how that impacts all of the mental health professions.

As stated earlier, I have tried to write each chapter to "stand alone." However, I urge you to read every chapter. You may be sure you want to be a psychologist so only look at that chapter and then miss what other helping professions are available. You don't know what you don't know! Your career is something you will be pursuing for your lifetime; take a couple of hours now to research exactly what you want that career to be.

Unit 1
Career Essentials

1

Ph.D. or Psy.D. in Clinical Psychology

Overall History and Philosophy of the Profession

There are several intersecting areas to discuss when trying to get an accurate taste of the history of psychology. In the following section I will note important and significant aspects of the early history of psychology, expand on the schools of thought that have emerged throughout the last century, discuss how the role of assessment in psychology developed, note significant history related to treatment issues, and relate a brief background regarding the development of the American Psychological Association (APA), psychology's national professional organization.

Early History

The role that most people are likely to associate with a mental health career is a psychologist. Indeed, psychology is one of the oldest mental health professions. As we begin to examine the history of psychology, understand first that there are theories and ideas of mental illness, and its treatment that can be traced back many centuries. For example, in medieval times, beliefs that evil spirits inhabited those who suffered from what may have been depression or psychosis were prominent, and many espoused the belief that hysteria in women was due to her uterus "wandering" throughout her body. These rather misguided

Careers in Mental Health: Opportunities in Psychology, Counseling, and Social Work,
First Edition. Kim Metz.
© 2016 John Wiley & Sons, Ltd. Published 2016 by John Wiley & Sons, Ltd.

ideas may represent some early understanding that people's experiences and thoughts have an influence on their behavior. However, it is widely accepted that the *general* discipline of psychology began in 1879, when Wilhelm Wundt started the first experimental laboratory in psychology at the University of Leipzig in Germany. Four years later, in 1883, G. Stanley Hall established a similar laboratory at Johns Hopkins University in the United States. These laboratories enabled the observation and manipulation of human mental processes using scientific methods. And they represent the beginning of the general discipline of psychology.

In 1896 Lightner Witmer founded the first psychology clinic at the University of Pennsylvania. This is considered the beginning of the branch of psychology referred to as *clinical* psychology. It should be noted that the *general* field of psychology has many branches. In fact, the APA identifies 54 divisions of psychology (http://www.apa.org/about/division/index.aspx). Examples include experimental psychology, cognitive psychology, forensic psychology, and industrial/organization psychology, to name just a few. This text will not expand on these branches of the psychology profession as, while they all involve "helping people," it is not through face-to-face therapy or counseling, in which most readers of this text likely have the most interest. There are very good texts available that examine the various branches of psychology and the educational track that one would follow to pursue them. You are urged to check those out if you want to research other ways that psychology helps people. The branches of psychology in which you likely are most interested are clinical psychology, counseling psychology (discussed further in Chapter 2), and school psychology (discussed further in Chapter 7).

Schools of Thought

As already stated, the opening of Witmer's psychology clinic represents the beginning of clinical psychology. However, Sigmund Freud's contributions in the area of psychoanalysis and the psychodynamic theory probably shone the brightest spotlight on the field. He believed that people were motivated by unconscious motives and drives and that their childhood experiences and crises were vital to understanding their adult personality. He also suggested that personality development occurred due to children passing through his proposed stages of psychosexual development. Freud's theories were (and are) quite controversial, and many people minimize the validity of his theory. However, what is important for clinical psychologists and other mental health providers is that, regardless of one's view of Freud's ideas, he was instrumental in proposing that not all mental problems have physiological causes. Prior to Freud and Witmer, the prevailing belief represented a more biological view (or medical model view) of mental processes. That is, all behavior had its origin in something biological versus environmental. While it is now quite accepted that biology plays a substantial role in one's mental health, it is also known that the environment and personal characteristics play a role too.

Freud also used psychoanalysis to treat his patients. Psychoanalysis could be viewed as the beginning of "talk therapy." In psychoanalysis the therapist or psychoanalyst explores the patient's view of his/her past or childhood and uses hypnosis and dream interpretation to uncover unconscious drives or explanations for present behavior. While some of his techniques might be considered extreme by many therapists today, it is an unavoidable conclusion that Freud's ideas have influenced modern-day talk therapy.

Before we delve any deeper into the important historical events that shaped psychology, let us examine the schools of thought that developed after Freud's psychoanalytical or psychodynamic approach. Briefly, the other main theories that would emerge in the next half century were behaviorism, cognitive psychology, and humanist psychology. Ultimately, these schools of thought influenced not only psychologists but also each of the mental health professions. So, to continue, let us examine the development of these schools of thought.

As explained earlier, Freud's psychodynamic perspective was one of the initial ways that psychologists tried to explain clients' behavior and psychological difficulties. However, soon another theory would challenge Freud's ideas. In 1913 John B. Watson began work that would eventually be categorized as the school of thought referred to as behaviorism. He and his followers rejected the emphasis Freud and his colleagues put on unconscious (and therefore, unobservable) forces and drives. They felt strongly that a person's behavior – not a person's unconscious or childhood traumas – was the key to understanding that person. Since the unconscious was not measurable or observable, the behaviorists felt there was no place for it in psychological theory. Instead, researchers such as B.F. Skinner concentrated on operant conditioning, which emphasized the effect that consequences and reinforcements had on a person's behavior. Behaviorism had a major impact on the field of psychology for quite some time. Many concepts from it can be seen in use today (e.g., token economies, behavior modification). The behaviorist idea that consequences and reinforcements can change behavior is still a powerful idea in psychology as well as other mental health professions.

Cognitive psychology emerged in the mid-1950s. It is part of a larger field termed cognitive science that is interdisciplinary in nature and can include the fields of linguistics, anthropology, neuroscience, philosophy, and education as well as psychology. Proponents of cognitive psychology, partially in response to the emphasis on behaviorism, believe that internal processes (thoughts, ideas, values, memories) could mediate behavior. That is, behavior is maintained not only by consequences and reinforcement but also by individuals' thoughts and expectations. For example, even if rewarded handsomely for a task some people will turn down the task because it violates a value that they strongly hold. One of the more influential theories from this school of thought was Jean Piaget's theory of cognitive development in which he delineates stages of cognitive development that children pass through en route to attaining their adult level of cognition and thought. If you haven't had a course in human development involving Piaget and his theory, do a quick Internet search and briefly examine his stages of development.

Also in the mid-1950s another school of thought was emerging. Psychologists such as Carl Rogers and Abraham Maslow felt that psychoanalysis and behaviorism assumed more negative about people than positive. They felt that people were not simply slaves to their unconscious drives nor were they puppets that could be controlled by rewards and consequences. Instead, humanists propose that individuals are able to exercise free choice and that each person has a potential they strive to realize. The basic belief of those who reside in the humanist camp is that humans are innately good and that they are capable of expressing free will and striving for self-actualization. Therapists who operate from a humanist perspective believe that if they treat clients with unconditional positive regard and allow the client – rather than the therapist – be the authority on their own inner experience, the client will achieve effective change. This type of therapy is often termed client-centered therapy.

Now that we have summarized the basic schools of thought that have shaped and continue to shape the mental health professions, let's go back and note some other important occurrences in the growth of psychology.

Psychological Assessment

The scope of clinical psychology was broadened in 1905 to include the conducting of psychological assessments. There are various types of assessments utilized by psychologists; for example, intelligence tests, aptitude tests, and personality tests. A more detailed explanation of the history of intelligence testing can be found in the history section of Chapter 7 (School Psychologist). Briefly, know that first, Alfred Binet and Theodore Simon developed what is now (after several refinements by others) the intelligence test or IQ test, which is purported to measure general intelligence. An IQ test is administered individually and the results are reported as a numerical score. An average score is 100 and the standard deviation of these tests is 15. On the other hand, aptitude tests (such as the ACT and SAT or the military ASVAB exam) measure one's likely future ability to be proficient in a particular area or at a particular skill. These tests (while not without their flaws) began to get widespread use in the military during World War I and later in World War II. They were utilized to assist in the placement of soldiers into the most appropriate job duty.

Later, in 1921, Hermann Rorschach developed his personality test, the Rorschach inkblot test. His test and other personality inventories and tests that followed were designed to measure a person's traits or characteristics that are stable across various situations. As stated, the advent of this type of measurement of human potential and personality opened many more doors for psychologists. Moreover, assessment and testing – intelligence, aptitude, and personality testing, among others – are one of the skills in the purview of clinical psychologists as well as school psychologists (Chapter 7). They continue to be one of the niches that make psychology different from some of the other mental health careers. That is, while other mental health professions may be trained in the use of a limited number of assessment measures, only psychologists are trained and licensed to conduct and interpret the results of all psychological assessment measures.

Treatment Issues

Another important thing that helped shaped psychology (as well as other mental health professions) was that in 1900 Clifford Beers, a Yale graduate who was employed in the insurance industry, made a suicide attempt, was hospitalized and diagnosed with manic depression. He found the conditions inside the mental institution in which he was housed deplorable. He wrote letters while in the hospital to state officials and then, in 1903 after he had been released, he wrote a book titled *A Mind That Found Itself*, which detailed the problems he saw inside the institution. The book was widely read and led to reforms in the way mentally ill people were treated. Beers' work helped call more attention to the mental health movement and subsequently mental health workers and their training.

It was decades later, in 1963, when another event helped shape the treatment of patients and the practice of psychology and, as you will read in subsequent chapters, the practice of other mental health professions. President John F. Kennedy signed the Community Mental Health Centers Construction Act, which mandated federal funds for the creation of mental health centers around the country. The idea was to be able to provide community-based care as an alternative to institutionalization. This obviously opened up more job opportunities for mental health professionals.

Incidentally, Kennedy's vision was never fully realized. The intention was noble. While the deplorable conditions that Beers wrote about in the early 1900s did not exist in the 1950s, there was still a great deal of patients housed and likely medicated long-term in mental hospitals. For example, the average length of stay for someone diagnosed with schizophrenia was 11 years. While state hospital admissions declined by 90% after the act was passed, only about half of the proposed mental health centers were ever built, and none were fully funded. Some believe that ultimately a disservice was done to the mentally ill. Former U.S. Representative Patrick Kennedy (the nephew of President Kennedy) stated in 2013 as the 50th anniversary of the act was observed, "The goals of deinstitutionalization were perverted. People who did need institutional care got thrown out, and there weren't the programs in place to keep them supported." He continued, "We don't have an alternate policy to address the needs of the severely mentally ill" ("Kennedy's vision"). As you contemplate your potential contributions to the mental health field, keep in mind this very real problem of the underserved mentally ill.

Treatment issues have more recently been affected by the advent of managed care and the influence of insurance companies in general in the medical/psychological fields. Because these issues have a strong impact on not only psychologists but also on all the other mental health professions, I have chosen to discuss them in more depth in Unit 2. Let it suffice to say here that the ways that professionals are reimbursed for their services have an impact on treatment.

Professional Organization – the APA

As you will realize when you examine each of the subsequent chapters regarding other professions, the development of a field is often related to the development and strength of a professional organization that helps to unify individuals in the field and standardize details such as the training of students in the field. Psychology is no different. In 1892 the American Psychological Association (APA) was founded by a group of 31 men who elected G. Stanley Hall as its first president. Membership in the organization grew slowly but, by 1940, there were over 600 members. However, in the late 1920s the APA expanded its membership to include what it termed associate members. Associate members did not possess Ph.D.s but were doing applied work (the kind many of you hope to do) with individuals. Growth in this type of membership soared, reaching just over 2,000 by 1940.

The inclusion of associate members in the APA represented a combining of *general* psychology, which involved engaging in and embracing scientific process as well as conducting research, and *applied* psychology, which involved working directly with people in order to help them overcome personal difficulties. Further merging of these two aspects of psychology within the APA occurred during World War II, when the APA leaders reorganized and merged with other psychological organizations that existed at the time. The mission of the APA was now not just promoting the practice of the science of psychology but also advancing the application of psychology and promoting human welfare. This dual emphasis remains today.

When World War II ended psychology enjoyed its greatest growth. With servicemen returning home, there was a need for a variety of services that psychologists could provide. Issues ranged from reunification with family to coping with traumatic war memories to assisting with reentering the civilian workforce. Psychology was enjoying a surge in growth, credibility, and financial funding. Similarly, the APA was growing. Membership grew from 4,000 in 1945 to 30,000 in 1970.

It was around this time that the APA also began to design a divisional structure within its organization. That is, once an APA member, the psychologist could choose to join one or more of several "special interest" divisions. The most popular divisions at the time were Clinical (now, Division 12) and Personnel, which is now called Counseling (Division 17). As mentioned earlier in this chapter, there is a total of 54 divisions in the APA today. While the breadth of interest areas attracts more members and illustrates the versatility of psychology, some fear that the divisions fragment the discipline and make members less unified.

As you can see, the field of psychology has undergone a great deal of growth in its comparatively short history. I have tried to give you a flavor of that growth by examining the early history of the field, the role of assessment measures, the changes in treatment venues, and the development of a professional organization to attempt to unify professionals in the field. As you read about other mental health professions you will see how some of the same influences expanded upon here have had an effect on their profession too.

Education

Let me begin with some generalities about graduate training in psychology. In general, in order to become a psychologist, one needs to complete a doctoral program. This typically involves about 4–5 years of graduate study and a 1-year internship. Sometimes programs will award a master's degree along the way (after 2 years of coursework and the completion of a master's thesis) but this degree is not meant as a stopping point (more about the perils of stopping with a master's degree in psychology at the end of this chapter). Rather, the terminal or final intended degree is the doctoral degree or Ph.D. (or Psy.D., which will be discussed further later in this chapter). As part of the coursework, students are expected to complete a dissertation. The parameters of the dissertation will vary based on the type of program in which the student is enrolled. However, at its basic level, a dissertation is a piece of original research in which one does an extensive review of the literature in a particular area, then designs a study that might be a logical "next step" for that particular area of interest. After the proposed study is approved, the actual study would be carried out, statistical analysis would be conducted and interpretations of the data would be made and analyzed. This is a lengthy and rather lonely process but goes a long way to prove that the graduate is able to synthesize, analyze, and think scientifically about information.

As stated above, there is always a requirement of a 1-year internship. The internship is coordinated with the Association of Psychology Postdoctoral and Internship Center (APPIC). Students may apply to internships with members of the APPIC. Once students apply they are "matched" by the APPIC. This process is a somewhat stressful one as there are a limited number of APPIC sites, and students are likely to be applying to locations out of state. At times students are not matched with a site and have to wait a year to apply again or use the APPIC Clearinghouse to obtain a site that may not have been their first choice. When applying to both graduate programs and/or internships, students are strongly encouraged to only apply to ones that have been granted accreditation by the APA to ensure that the programs meet basic standards it sets forth.

There are four routes to earning a doctoral degree in a branch of psychology that conducts psychotherapy or assessment. These are

- a Ph.D. in clinical psychology
- a Ph.D. in counseling psychology
- a Psy.D. in clinical or
- a Psy.D. in counseling psychology.

Counseling psychology will be discussed further in the next chapter. However, at this time I want to explain more about the differences between a Ph.D. and a Psy.D. In order to understand the distinctions between these degrees, a bit more history and context is needed. As was briefly discussed in the history section, following World War II there was an influx of veterans experiencing psychological difficulties, especially symptoms of what we now term post-traumatic stress syndrome. Therefore, the federal government increased the funding granted to clinical psychology graduate programs, and the Veterans Administration (VA) provided sites for those students to practice their clinical skills. This quick growth of clinical psychology caused many to question exactly how students were being trained. As a result, in 1949, the APA held the Boulder Conference on Graduate Education in Clinical Psychology in Boulder, Colorado.

Prior to this, the prevailing philosophy of training was much the same as it was for other disciplines (e.g., history, philosophy, etc.). That is, that graduate students would become versed in scientific inquiry and use their skills to further the knowledge base of the discipline through scientific research. While this was seen as a noble and certainly a typical goal of earning an advanced degree, many in the field of psychology felt that training programs were neglecting the applied goal of teaching students how to work with and counsel people. Therefore, the purpose of the Boulder Conference was to determine the best way to train psychologists. Based on the discussions at the conference it was decided that students would be taught to conduct and to critically examine research in the discipline but would also learn more hands-on applied clinical skills. This model drove and continues to drive most clinical psychology programs. These are programs in which the graduate is awarded a Ph.D. This model came to be termed the Boulder model or the scientist/practitioner model as graduates would learn the skills of a scientist as well as the skills of a practicing therapist.

However, many were not satisfied with the philosophy of the Boulder model. Critics believed that the emphasis on research was too great. Indeed, many students labored through the research portion of their graduate program (often including completing a thesis and dissertation) with no real desire or intention to use those research skills in their career, as their plan was to engage in more applied, therapeutic work. Therefore, in 1974 at another APA conference held in Vail, Colorado, an APA committee proposed a second model of training. This model, known as the Vail model or practitioner model, emphasizes the practitioner portion of training over the scientist. The philosophy was that students would receive a *professional degree* more akin to the degree earned by lawyers and doctors who attend law school and medical school versus receiving an *academic degree* more akin to the degree earned by other academics, such as, those who receive Ph.D.s in philosophy, English, economics, and so on. Indeed, programs might not even be housed in a university but could be in freestanding schools. The degree awarded to graduates would be a Psy.D.

It was agreed that both models, the Boulder model or Ph.D. and the Vail model or Psy.D., would provide viable ways to be trained and later practice psychology. Today, graduates of both types of programs are qualified for the same clinically oriented jobs. The major difference is that only the Ph.D. graduates would likely be qualified for full-time, tenure-track employment at a college or university. Most of those positions require the research background that the Ph.D. training includes. Part-time or adjunct teaching may be viable options for the Psy.D., depending on the university.

While the Psy.D. is a legitimate way to earn the title of clinical psychologist, graduates did initially face some resistance from professionals in the field (all of whom held Ph.D.s) and were perhaps seen as holding a lesser degree. However, those attitudes have softened.

Main Differences Between Ph.D. and Psy.D.

The distinctions between the two programs, Ph.D. and Psy.D., are often difficult to discern. The easiest way to flesh out some of the distinctions and differences is to list them for you. So, the following list compares the Ph.D. and Psy.D. in various categories.

- Dissertation: While both programs take at least 4 years (often closer to 5–7 years) to complete coursework and culminate in a year-long internship, only Ph.D. programs require a research-based dissertation. For a dissertation, a student typically designs a study, proposes it to a committee comprising graduate professors, then once approved by them collects and gathers data, analyzes the data using statistical procedures, and finally interprets that data. It is intended that the student's project will help further the knowledge base in the area of psychology. On the other hand, while Psy.D. students also complete a culminating project, it is not necessarily a research-based scientific study (though it could be) but may be more community-based or more qualitative than quantitative. Due to the length of time needed to complete a more scientifically based study, often students in a Ph.D. program may take longer to finish their doctoral program.

- Stigma: As mentioned earlier there is a softened stigma, though stigma nonetheless, toward Psy.D.s by Ph.D.s. The negative view may be more pronounced if the student graduated from a free-standing versus a university-based Psy.D. program. Presumably this is because the freestanding schools have higher enrollment numbers and therefore possibly less stringent admission require-ments, and because their students are often not required to complete a research-based dissertation. Despite the negative views that Ph.D.s may hold, it should be pointed out that those views end with them. That is, the general public and insurance companies see the two degrees as equivalent. So clients will rarely request one degreed professional over another, and insur-ance companies pay the same for psychologists who hold either degree. Additionally, according to data provided by the APPIC, there is no substantial difference between degrees in terms of acceptance to internship.

- Admissions and debt: The biggest difference between Ph.D.s and Psy.D.s is the admissions process into their schools and the level of financial aid offered by both. Ph.D. programs typically have fund-ing for their incoming students, so that students leave with less debt than they might incur in Psy.D. programs. Ph.D. programs can do this for two reasons. First, since they are all part of universi-ties, their professors are doing their own research and often bring-ing in grant dollars – which can be filtered to funding for incoming students. Second and more significant for you, the reader, is that Ph.D. programs accept far fewer students and therefore have more rigorous admission criteria. Thus, it is much more difficult to get accepted to a Ph.D. program but, once in, you will accrue much less debt. Alternatively, it is easier to get accepted to a

Psy.D. program but you will accrue much more debt in the process as there is less funding available.

- Graduate coursework: Coursework in a Ph.D. program will include more classes in research methods and statistics than a Psy.D. program. However, keep in mind that Psy.D.s are still being trained to understand and digest research. It is important for everyone to be adept at comprehending the most recent studies being conducted. However, the Ph.D. will also be learning how to conduct the research. For a discussion on the importance of research, please refer to Box 1.1. Beyond that, both types of programs will have classes in assessing, diagnosing, and treating mental illness. Psy.D. programs may have more practicum or hands-on training opportunities. Bear in mind, however, every program is unique and when students are applying they should be attending to what is emphasized and what is not in order to help determine the best fit for them.

- Internship: Recall that after 4–5 years of coursework, students must complete an internship. One way to judge the differences between Ph.D. and Psy.D programs is to look at APPIC internship acceptance rates. According to the APPIC summary of internship match rates (http://www.appic.org/Portals/0/downloads/APPIC_Match_Rates_2011-14_by_State.pdf) there are some differences in acceptance rates. The APPIC gives a summary of match rates for the combined years of 2011–2014. It reports that overall during those years 79% of Ph.D. candidates were matched with an internship. While 70% of Psy.D. candidates were matched with an internship. These numbers become more disparate when you look at the type of internships to which they were accepted. That is, of the 79% of Ph.D. candidates who were matched to an internship, 91% were matched to an *APA accredited* internship. Of the 70% of Psy.D. candidates who were matched to an internship, 57% were matched to an *APA-accredited* internship. The link to the report referenced above also gives the statistics for individual programs. It is possible to find a particular Psy.D. program with higher APA-accredited acceptance rates than another particular Ph.D. program. Therefore, when looking at graduate schools, be sure to check the rates for the program you are interested in and see how they compare to other programs.

Box 1.1   Why is Research so Important?

Many high school and undergraduate students hear teachers and professionals extol the virtues of conducting research. You may wonder why it's so important or so emphasized. First, the job of those who work in higher education is not just to educate students but also to contribute to the knowledge base of the profession. For example, how does one know how brain functioning contributes to depression or why certain treatments work better than others or whether there is enough evidence to call a certain set of symptoms a new disorder or what is the best way to interview a child who is suspected of being sexually abused? Of course, rigorous scientific research is needed to help answer such questions. "That's fine," you say. "Let someone else do the research, I just want to do therapy." While that is understandable, please remember that, in order to treat individuals with mental health issues, you need to at least read, digest, and evaluate the research in those areas just mentioned. That means you need some working knowledge of research methods and statistics so that you can discern whether any given research finding is valid. There have been many ill-conceived treatments that were not scientifically validated but used by clinicians and subsequently had very detrimental effects on clients. Look up "rebirthing therapy" or "facilitated communication" or "use of anatomically correct dolls in assessing sexual abuse." These treatments or techniques have illustrated the perils of not conducting scientific research properly AND the perils of professionals not understanding that the treatments were problematic because they were unable to critically evaluate the claims of those who developed or designed the treatment.

- Licensing: Both degreed professionals will have to sit for the Examination for the Professional Practice of Psychology (EPPP), which will be discussed further in the next section. Another way to look at the distinctions between the two professions is to examine the average "pass" rate on this exam of both types of graduates. The Association of State and Provincial Psychology

Boards (ASPPB) publishes a report each year detailing how each program (clinical, counseling, Ph.d., Psy.D) performs on the exam. The most recent report was published in 2012 and included data detailing the pass rate of test takers from 2007 to 2012. You can find the report in its entirety at http://c.ymcdn. com/sites/www.asppb.net/resource/resmgr/EPPP_/2012_ ASPPB_Exam_Scores_by_Do.pdf.

You can use the information in the tables to look at the doctoral programs in each state and determine the number of people who attempted the exam and the percentage who passed it. After examining the numbers the Social Psychology Network published on its website (https://www.socialpsychology.org/clinrank.htm) an ordering of the data organized by Jean M. Kim and Edward C. Chang from the University of Michigan. The data indicate that Ph.D. graduates typically perform at higher levels than Psy.D. graduates. Norcross (2000), who noted the same trend in previous decades, points out that this replicated difference may be due to the sizes of the programs. For example, smaller Ph.D. programs with higher faculty/ student ratios typically produce students who perform better on the exam than Ph.D. graduates from comparatively larger programs with lower faculty/student ratios. Therefore, since most Psy.D. programs are larger (though not all), their lower scores may be more a function of that characteristic than the underlying philosophy and training of the program. Either way, whichever program you choose, it is worth taking a look at the scores of the school's graduates on the EPPP as *one* measure of the strength of the program.

- Employment: As mentioned above, with the exception of tenure-track university faculty positions that a Psy.D. may have trouble securing, the two degrees will qualify graduates for the exact same types of positions.

Licensing

Following the completion of coursework and the internship, students will earn their doctoral degree (Ph.D. or Psy.D.). However, before graduates can begin independent practice they will have to first accrue a certain amount of supervised client hours and, second, sit for the

EPPP. Prior to passing this exam, a graduate may still work as a psychologist but must be supervised by a licensed psychologist.

Accruing supervised hours typically consists of weekly face-to-face meetings with a licensed psychologist on a weekly basis. During these meetings, the diagnosis, treatment, and/or progress of various clients whom the supervisee is seeing are discussed. The supervisor also needs to sign off on insurance forms. These supervised hours are typically required by each state before graduates can sit for the EPPP. Each state has a different amount of supervised client hours required.

The EPPP is administered by the Association of State and Provincial Licensing Boards (ASPLB) and consists of 225 multiple-choice questions; candidates are given 4 hours and 15 minutes to complete the exam. Each question has four choices and only one choice will be the correct one. There is no penalty for guessing. Interestingly, of the 225 questions, only 175 are scored. The other 50 are considered pre-test questions and, based on responses from candidates, may be included as a scored item on a future exam. The raw scores (which had been used in the past to determine cutoffs) are now converted to scaled scores. Therefore, scores will range from 200 to 800. This conversion to scaled scores enables administrators to take into consideration question difficulty and other test factors. That is, perhaps one version of the test is slightly more difficult than the one given the year before. The scaled scores help account for that. If you don't understand the reasoning behind the scaled scores, know that you will after you take your undergraduate course in statistics! In terms of passing the exam, each state has its own cutoff score. However, more than 90% of the jurisdictions that utilized the exam use 500 as a passing score. This is the score recommended by the ASPPB. In case you're curious, about 80% pass the exam on their first try.

Understand that this is an exam for which you will study. While the scoring is standardized like the score for the SAT, it is a different kind of test. The SAT was intended to be an aptitude test and was originally designed to measure your potential to do well in college. Despite the fact that there are study courses and books to buy to improve your SAT scores, most students do not score appreciably higher on subsequent administrations because their overall potential to do well in college doesn't change drastically. In fact, most of the classes and books focus on test-taking strategies versus increasing knowledge in a particular area. The EPPP is instead measuring actual knowledge about or achievement in understanding topics in psychology. Currently, that includes questions from the following areas: the biological bases of behavior, the cognitive-affective bases of behavior, the social and cultural bases of behavior, growth and lifespan development, assessment and diagnosis, treatment and intervention, research methods and statistics, and ethical and professional issues. There are materials you can purchase that streamline the tremendous knowledge base in these areas. Practice exams are typically included allowing you to gauge progress and try to increase knowledge in areas in which you test more poorly.

To summarize, licensing as a psychologist requires graduation from a doctoral program, completion of a state-mandated number of supervised hours with clients, and a passing score on the EPPP. Again, prior to the completion of these requirements, you may see clients but it will have to be under the supervision of a licensed psychologist.

Types of Jobs for which the Degree will Qualify You

Ph.D. and Psy.D. graduates are qualified for the same types of jobs (with the exception of college professor – this will be discussed at the end of this section). The following describes the type of sites where a clinical psychologist may work.

Inpatient Hospital

Inpatient units in a hospital and/or psychiatric hospitals house clients with severe mental health problems who may be a danger to themselves or others. Patients in these facilities may be there voluntarily or involuntarily. Due to insurance restrictions and the theory that patients should be kept in the "least restrictive environment" possible, stays are often not long in an inpatient ward. Among persons with serious mental illness, the average length of hospitalization declined from 12.8 to 9.7 days between 1995 and 2002 (Watanabe-Galloway & Zhang, 2007.) Therefore, while individual and group therapy may be a part of psychologists' duties on an inpatient unit, they will not likely engage in long-term therapeutic interventions. Their goal will be to stabilize and refer the patient to an outpatient agency for follow-up. Psychologists will play an integral role in the evaluation of the patient's status. They will likely be part of a treatment team composed of psychiatrists, social workers, and nurses who work together to design an appropriate treatment plan. One of the most significant contributions that the psychologist will make on an inpatient unit is to exercise his/her skill at psychological assessment. Psychologists will use intelligence and personality testing to help make determinations about an individual's mental state and capabilities as well as about their diagnosis and treatment plan.

Many hospitals will also have a partial hospitalization unit that they utilize as a "step down" for patients. Patients come to sessions for several hours a day, several days a week, but still live at home. This is more cost effective and affords the individual the ability to remain at home. Psychologists may be employed doing individual, group, or family therapy on a partial hospitalization unit.

Part of a Team at Another Type of Facility

Psychologists may also be employed as part of a treatment team at other types of agencies. For example, prisons, group homes, and nursing homes typically have a psychologist on staff. The psychologist will do individual, group, and family therapy, and consult with other professionals at the facility to help determine the best treatment plan for individuals in their care.

Outpatient Mental Health Clinic

Many psychologists work in outpatient mental health clinics conducting individual, group, marital, and/or family therapy. Additionally, they may perform psychological assessments using intelligence, personality and/or aptitude tests, and write reports detailing their results.

Private Practice

Many psychologists start their own private practice. While running one's own private practice is often viewed as a career goal, there is a great deal besides doing therapy that goes into it. These practitioners must also be versed in or get assistance in how to choose appropriate office space for a sound price, how to hire (and possibly fire) support staff to answer phones, greet clients, and file insurance claims. For this reason, I often recommend advisees consider a minor in business while they are still an undergraduate. Other psychologists may not own the private practice but work as an independent contractor in someone else's practice. In that capacity they hold no responsibility for the business side of the practice but see clients for therapy or assessment. They are typically paid a percentage of what the practice owner receives from insurance and/or client payments.

College Counseling Center

Hodges (2001) notes that, when college counseling centers were established in the early/mid-1900s, it was common practice for faculty members to counsel students about academic and, later, personal issues. Over time, with the solidification of both counseling psychology and mental health counseling, the role was eventually given to professionals with more training and specialization in counseling techniques.

Today, those professionals could be psychologists (clinical or counseling, Ph.D. or Psy.D.) or mental health counselors or social workers. Clients will be limited to students at the university in which the professional is employed. Presenting problems are often things that "traditional" students may be experiencing, such as homesickness, relationship issues, or vocational issues. However, students may also present with more severe psychological disturbances such as suicidal ideation or drug and/or alcohol abuse. Further, many college students are NOT "traditional" but adult students with families and careers so that therapists at a counseling center would have to be prepared to encounter as many presenting problems as someone in private practice or at a mental health center.

Additionally, campuses are more likely now than ever to be made up of a diverse population of students from various backgrounds and countries. So, those who work there must be adept at cross-cultural and diversity issues (Hodges, 2001). University counseling center personnel may also be called upon to present information to various campus organizations and/or do campus-wide programming. If you would like to peruse various job openings to see exactly what some counseling centers are looking for in their professional employees, try the Association for University and College Counseling Center Directors' website (http://www.aucccd.org/job-postings). The "job board" allows you to get familiar with what many schools look for in candidates for college counseling center positions.

Primary Practice Psychologist

A newer venue in which a psychologist may be employed is in a primary practice physician office, such as family practice office or a pediatrician office. The collaboration between physician and psychologist is sometimes referred to as integrated medical care. The exact role that each psychologist might play in a medical practice is varied and, really, still being defined (McDaniel & deGruy, 2014).

For example, psychologists may help with assessment and follow-up of clients who present to physicians with psychologically related issues such as depression or attention deficit disorder. Patients may turn to their family doctor or pediatrician for psychotropic medication for a couple of reasons. First, in areas where patients do not have easy access to psychiatrists, patients may rely on their family doctor or pediatrician for medication for psychological ailments. Second, patients may also choose to see their family doctor for psychotropic medication because they trust their family practice doctor more than a psychiatrist who they may feel is not as versed in their history. Though pediatricians and family practice doctors are well within their competence when they prescribe psychotropic medication, some acknowledge that it is advantageous to have a psychologist on staff to conduct assessments and confirm diagnoses before the physician prescribes for a psychological problem.

Alternatively, a psychologist may be part of a treatment team at the medical office that helps to make decisions about the care of a patient. Further, psychologists could be called upon to follow up with patients between appointments to help increase treatment compliance and track progress. As stated earlier, this is a very new area for psychologists (and perhaps other mental health professionals) to be employed. The APA has, however, already begun compiling lists of internships that provide specific training in the area of primary care.

Finally, I should note here that psychologists may be utilized one day to actually prescribe for patients in medical settings. A movement is afoot to advocate for psychologists to receive training and accreditation in prescribing psychotropic medications for clients. I will expand more on the possibility of psychologists having prescription privileges in Chapter 12.

University Professor

This is the one job category in which a Psy.D. will have a more difficult time working. Most universities require that their tenure-track faculty members hold a Ph.D. Because university professors are required not only to teach students but also to engage in research, their experience with their own thesis and dissertation and their likely collaboration with graduate faculty research while they were in graduate school are thought to make them more prepared for faculty positions. This Ph.D. requirement is not unique to psychology. Most undergraduate colleges will require faculty in all departments to hold a Ph.D. Therefore, if teaching is something in which you think you might be interested one day, you may need to be looking more at Ph.D. track jobs. Also, remember that if research is something that really interests you, there are other ways to do this besides earning a Ph.D. in *clinical* psychology. Students who get Ph.D.s in, for example, experimental psychology, cognitive psychology, or social psychology may have as their career goals teaching at the university level and engaging in research in their field. If a faculty position is something that you desire one day, keep in mind that the larger the university the more emphasis that will likely be placed on research. For example, you may have heard the phrase "publish or perish," meaning that if faculty members don't publish a sufficient amount of research in reputable journals they will not be granted tenure and will therefore likely need to find other employment. Other, often smaller schools, will still value and expect research production but will have less stringent requirements of their faculty.

Obviously, in addition to the research and scholarship just discussed, a faculty member will be required to teach a prescribed number of classes each semester, the number of which will vary from school to school and be based on the amount of research that is expected of the faculty. At larger research institutions with high expectations for faculty research, that number might only be two classes per semester. At smaller, liberal arts schools, it is usually closer to four. At community colleges where there is often no research requirement of faculty, the number could be as high as six. Often the salary of a professor of psychology will be lower than it would be if that person worked in the profession but outside of academia. However, there are usually other benefits in a university atmosphere, not the least of which includes a 9- or 10-month contract so that summers are freer.

Nursing Homes

Long-term care facilities for the elderly may have psychologists on staff to assist with mental health issues faced by the residents of the facility or to perform psychological assessments on the residents. In addition, the psychologist might also be charged with conducting training or workshops for the staff of the facility in order to help them better understand and interact with the residents who may be in varying stages of physical and mental decline.

This is a job site in which a psychologist could also work part time. There are various agencies that contract with long-term care facilities to provide a psychologist to visit a particular facility on a weekly or biweekly basis. The facility may not be able to afford a full-time psychologist and/or the facility may feel a weekly or biweekly visit from one is sufficient to meet the needs of its residents. Therefore, a psychologist could work for one of those contracting agencies and see clients/residents from one or more facilities each week.

Earning Potential

On average, psychologists will have higher earning potential than the other mental health professionals discussed in this book. This is due largely to the more advanced degree that they hold (a Ph.D. versus a master's). Insurance companies will reimburse more for a Ph.D. than they will for a master's level therapist. However, the difference is not substantial. As an example, at the private practice in which I work, Ph.D.s are paid 60% of whatever the practice owner collects for any given client. The master's level therapists (mental health counselors, social workers) typically start at 50% and move to 55% when they are completely licensed. Keep in mind that, as mentioned above, the amount paid by insurance providers to a Ph.D. is slightly higher than a master's level therapist. So the Ph.D. is receiving 60% of a slightly higher rate. Obviously, the hourly rate that is paid for a client hour will vary, but if you live in an area with an average cost of living you can guesstimate between $80 and $120 per hour. Before you start calculating a yearly income based on these numbers PLEASE read the information regarding salary in Unit 2 that discusses some of the reasons to and not to work in mental health. Spoiler alert: Getting rich is NOT one of the reasons to work in this field.

Of course, there are other types of jobs that a Ph.D. might hold that are not based on a "client hour" but on a salary that the agency, the hospital, the school, etc., may pay. This will vary based on the area in which you live. For each chapter I am going to give you some rough numbers based on the *Occupational Outlook Handbook* published by the U.S. Department of Labor. Overall, in 2012, the most recent data reported, the median salary for a psychologist was $69,280. The median salary is the wage that one half of those in the profession earned more than and one half of those in the profession earned less than. The numbers from the *Handbook* will be used to describe salary in subsequent chapters as well. This is a good way to compare "apples to apples." However, you have to remember that the number does not consider the area of the country in which one resides nor does it consider whether psychologists are just beginning their career or is late in their career. Again, though, the median salary gives you some perspective and a way to compare professions.

Types of Clients Served

Psychologists can work with a wide variety of clients. They are trained to conduct individual, group, family, and marital therapy. They may work with clients who suffer from depression, bipolar disorder, anxiety disorders, autism spectrum disorders, substance abuse disorders, psychotic disorders, and adjustment disorders, among others. They may work with prisoners or do crisis intervention after a traumatic event. Keep in mind that all mental health professionals must be sure to operate within their "scope of practice" or within areas in which they have competency. Therefore, not every psychologist may have the experience or specific training to deal with every issue. For example, while all psychologists will learn about family systems and family dynamics, they may not all have taken specific classes in marriage counseling. Therefore, that may not be one of the treatment modalities that they use. Another example of this is that, while all psychologists take classes in child and adolescent development and psychopathology, they did not all choose to do practicum or internship experience with children. Therefore, they may not see children and/or adolescents in their practice. Typically, the internship year is a time when experience is gained with specific populations. However, there are also plenty of "hands on" opportunities during graduate school in the form of practicum experience gained in facilities within the community and supervised by a faculty member. Following graduate school and licensure, psychologists must also do continuing education each year and will often take classes/workshops that will help them become more specialized in a particular area or with a particular population.

What about Getting a Master's Degree in Psychology?

I am including an extra section here because many students want to know about the advantages of earning a master's degree in clinical psychology – especially because in many programs graduates earn a master's as part of their journey to obtain a Ph.D. The answer to the question depends somewhat upon the state in which you reside. However, as a general rule of thumb, a master's in clinical psychology is not a useful degree because a master's level student is not eligible to apply for a license. He or she can practice but will always have to rely on a supervisor to sign off on treatment plans and insurance paperwork. There are a couple of exceptions.

First, a few states offer a license at the master's level. In most cases, the license does not allow you to refer to yourself as a "psychologist" but as one of a number of variations in titles. This will likely mean that your job responsibilities are reduced from that in which a psychologist might engage. States will use titles for their master's level clinicians such as Psychological Associate, Psychological Examiner, Psychological

Assistant, or Psychological Practitioner. States that offer a license in one of these areas are Alaska, Arkansas, California, Kentucky, Maine, Nebraska, New Mexico, Oregon, and Vermont. My information was gleaned from the ASPPB's website. Its site includes a link to the *Handbook of Licensing and Certification Requirements* (http://www.asppb.org/HandbookPublic/handbookreview.aspx). At this link you can view the licensing requirements for each state.

We have not yet discussed license-eligible mental health careers such as social work and counseling. However, these professions, as you will soon read, have different licensing rules and standards, and practitioners can therefore be licensed with a master's degree and do counseling with clients. They are generally referred to as LPCCs (Licensed Professional Clinical Counselors) or some variation of that. I bring this up because there are a few states that will also license master's level psychologists – not as psychologists, but as licensed professional clinical counselors. If this is an option you wish to explore, please be sure to check the rules of the state in which you live. In this case you would be looking up the rules for the state board of counseling to see if it includes provisions for master's level psychologists.

A second reason that some students pursue a master's in clinical psychology is because they have been turned down for admission to Ph.D. programs. They hope that earning a master's degree, and thereby gaining both research and clinical experience, will increase their attractiveness to Ph.D. programs when they reapply. The disadvantage to this is that, even if they are accepted to a Ph.D. program after their master's degree, the Ph.D. program will not automatically accept credit hours from the master's program. Therefore, students may find that they have to take 2 years to complete their master's program and still another 4 years if/when they get into their desired Ph.D. program.

References

Hodges, S. (2001). University counseling centers at the twenty-first century: Looking forward, looking back. *Journal of College Counseling*, 4(2), 161–173.

Kennedy's vision for mental health never realized. (2013, October 20). *USA Today*. Retrieved from http://www.usatoday.com/story/news/nation/2013/10/20/kennedys-vision-mental-health/3100001/.

McDaniel, S. H., & deGruy, F. V. (2014). An introduction to primary care and psychology. *American Psychologist,* 69, 325–331.

Norcross, J. C. (2000). Clinical v. counseling psychology: What's the diff? *Eye on Psi Chi,* 5(1), 20–22.

Occupational outlook handbook (2014–15 ed.). Washington, DC: Bureau of Labor Statistics, U.S. Department of Labor.

Watanabe-Galloway, S., & Zhang, W. (2007). Analysis of US trends in discharges from general hospitals for episodes of serious mental illness, 1995–2002. *Psychiatric Services,* 58(4), 496–502.

2

Ph.D. or Psy.D. in Counseling Psychology

Overall History and Philosophy of the Profession

As mentioned in the previous chapter, another way to obtain a doctorate in psychology is to earn a Ph.D. or Psy.D. in *counseling* psychology. This route creates yet more confusion for many undergraduate students in terms of distinguishing it from graduating with a Ph.D. in *clinical* psychology. Further, the two degrees involve similar training and enable individuals to perform similar jobs. In fact, at several junctures in their history, many have advocated for a merging of the two fields (Norcross, 2000). In this section, the substantial number of similarities and the most significant differences will be discussed.

The differences between the two professions are mainly related to history and philosophy. However, the historical differences that you see become very watered down as time goes on, and the differences today are much less substantial. History is still examined because it is productive to look at where a profession began in order to appreciate where it is now.

Counseling psychology itself has a shorter history than clinical psychology. Munley, Duncan, McDonnell, and Sauer published a brief history of counseling psychology in 2004. In it they note that Donald Super (1955) describes, "rather suddenly in 1951, a new job title, counseling psychologist, and a new field of psychology, counseling

Careers in Mental Health: Opportunities in Psychology, Counseling, and Social Work, First Edition. Kim Metz.

psychology, were born in the U.S." While the formal title was not used until the early 1950s, there were significant events from the previous 50 years that helped shape the profession of counseling psychology. Many of these events were rooted in the idea of vocational counseling.

For example, during the Industrial Revolution, when the availability of vocations increased dramatically beyond traditional agricultural work, Frank Parsons in 1908 opened the Vocation Bureau in Boston. Parsons is considered the father of vocational guidance, and he sought to help immigrants as well as current U.S. residents find appropriate work environments. He utilized psychometric instruments to assist individuals in their career choices. The subsequent Great Depression heightened the need for individuals to explore and find useful work.

Further, World War II contributed to the birth of counseling psychology in two ways. First, recall (from Chapter 1) that intelligence and aptitude tests had been developed so that soldiers leaving to fight for their country could be tested and assessed to see in what role they could be most useful, given their skills and interests. This type of vocational testing is still used extensively today for new military recruits. Second, when World War II soldiers returned home they needed to seek and find gainful employment after being out of the traditional workforce for several years. The Veterans Administration (VA) realized the employment needs of the returning soldier and began to look to clinical psychologists, who at the time worked mostly in hospital settings, to fill positions at the VA. They were needed not only to assist with job training and placement but to help veterans with overall life adjustment after the war. However, there were more openings at the VA than clinical psychologists to fill them. Recall that at this time, the clinical psychology training programs had just undergone great scrutiny and changes due to the Boulder model of training being adopted. Since their programs were strong, VA officials suggested that, if the APA's Division 17 (Counseling and Guidance) adopted similar training requirements as Division 12 (Clinical), jobs would be readily available for their graduates at VA facilities. This indeed occurred and, in 1952, the VA was the first agency to create the job title of "counseling psychologist" (Meara & Myers, 1999).

In 1958 the National Defense Education Act (NDEA) was passed. It was passed due to Cold War anxieties, which were heightened by the Soviet Union launching *Sputnik*, making it the first country to venture into space. Worried that the Soviet Union was surpassing the United States in space exploration, the act granted funds to schools to, among other things, hire guidance counselors. The hope was that these counselors would encourage young people to consider careers in the sciences (Meara & Myers, 1999). Often these counselors were teachers seeking to extend their education. Using funds from the NDEA, they enrolled in counseling and guidance programs or counseling psychology programs, which were often housed in education departments within universities.

Another important historical influence on counseling psychology was the passage of the Community Mental Health Centers Construction Act of 1963. It granted federal funds for the creation and development of community mental health centers. This actually propelled all mental health professions forward, but for counseling psychology it had another positive effect. It allowed for agencies to spend time and money on prevention and outreach. Prevention and outreach, along with assessment, interest in normal development, and group and individual counseling, were activities seen as integral to counseling psychologists' mission.

As has been noted, the APA was founded by G. Stanley Hall in 1892. During the ensuing few decades, various interest groups or divisions developed within and outside the APA (Munley et al., 2004) with the intent to draw together individuals with certain specialty interests. In the 1940s, a major restructuring and reorganization of those groups took place. Psychologists were polled to determine major areas of interest in the discipline. The survey found that the highest interest was for clinical psychology and the second highest for personnel psychology. Further, many professionals "wrote in" that they believed guidance was also a high-interest category. Therefore, when the APA reorganized its divisions in the mid-1940s, Division 12 was defined as Clinical Psychology and Division 17 was termed Personnel and Guidance. Many began to use the terms counseling and personnel interchangeably, so eventually Division 17 became known as Counseling and Guidance.

In 1951, Division 17 sponsored the Northwestern Conference on the Training of Counseling Psychologists. This is when the term counseling psychology was first used. Participants attempted to discern roles of and appropriate training for counseling psychologists. Many of the education guidelines that were proposed followed closely how clinical psychologists were being trained, including having an emphasis on research as well as practice. At this time, the name of the division was also changed to Counseling Psychology. Munley et al. (2004) quote directly from the APA report in reference to what the role and function of a counseling psychologist would be:

> The professional goal of the counseling psychologist is to foster the psychological development of the individual. This includes all people on the adjustment continuum from those who function at tolerable levels of adequacy to those suffering from more severe psychological disturbances. The counseling psychologist will spend the bulk of his time with individuals within the normal range, but his training should qualify him to work in some degree with individuals at any level of psychological adjustment. Counseling stresses the positive and preventive. (APA, 1952a, p. 175)

In 1967 another conference, termed the Greystone Conference, focused on the training of counseling psychologists. Additionally, the similarities between counseling psychology and clinical psychology were debated. It was thought that counseling psychology could take two directions. First, it could become a sub-specialty to clinical psychology. Second, it could strive to remain distinct from clinical and other areas of psychology (Altmaier & Hansen, 2011). We know now that counseling psychology retained its identity and its focus on prevention, on issues that normal/typical people face, and on understanding and appreciating lifespan development. The conference served as a way to clarify issues related to the identity of the profession and to project confidence in and elevate the status of the counseling profession (Vera, 2012).

In the 1970s and 1980s, the profession continued to grow. The number of graduate school programs increased from 27 in 1980 to 44 in 1985 and 59 in 1990. Additionally, in the late 1980s, Congress passed legislation that enabled psychologists to be reimbursed for their health care services. This prompted more counseling psychologists to go into private practice, further blurring the lines between clinical and counseling psychologists. Some began to worry that the things that made counseling more unique were becoming less prominent.

In 1987, counseling psychology held another national conference in Atlanta, Georgia, where five major issues were considered. They included taking another look at the public image of counseling psychology, examining professional practice in various settings, firming up training and accreditation standards, discussing research opportunities, and considering organizational and political issues in counseling psychology. Small work groups were formed to address each issue, and their conclusions were published in *The Counseling Psychologist* in 1988 (Rude, Weissberg, & Gazda, 1988). In that report, recommendations were made for counseling psychologists, for the APA and specifically Division 17, for university training programs, and for agencies offering internships and practicums. The recommendations included ways to continue to increase the quality of training and ways to support counseling psychology as a unique profession (Munley et al., 2004).

In this section, I have summarized the history of counseling psychology and tried to delineate some of the ways that this history sets the two professions apart. As you can see, there is a distinction between clinical and counseling psychology, and the distinction was more obvious years ago. That is, counseling psychologists spend more time with individuals experiencing normal psychological adjustment and in preventing psychological distresses. Clinical psychologists, on the other hand, spend more time treating people with abnormal psychological issues. As stated early in this section, though, those differences today are very minimal.

There are a few other practical differences between the professions that Norcross (2000) delineates. The first is the number of graduate programs that exist: The number of clinical programs exceeds the number of counseling programs. According to the APA website's listing of accredited doctoral programs in 2014, there are 71 accredited counseling psychology programs (66 offering Ph.D.s and 5 offering Psy.D.s) compared with 240 accredited clinical psychology programs (175 offering Ph.D.s and 65 offering Psy.D.s). The second difference concerns where within universities the programs are housed. Clinical psychology programs are most often housed in psychology departments, while counseling psychology programs can more often be found in education departments. This reflects the history of the two professions being based originally in psychology versus vocation and education. Finally, in terms of employment, while both professions are qualified for the same jobs, clinical psychologists seem to gravitate more to private practice and teaching positions at universities, and counseling psychologist are more often found in university counseling centers.

Education

The educational path for a counseling psychologist is very similar to that of the clinical psychologist. Therefore, be sure to examine the section on Education in Chapter 1, as much of this is expanded on there and I hesitate to simply duplicate it here. Briefly, after earning an undergraduate degree one would need to obtain a doctoral degree in counseling psychology. This can take anywhere from 5 to 7 years to complete. The program to which you apply should be accredited by the APA to ensure quality and breadth and depth of training. Again, similar to the clinical graduate programs, the culminating project in the doctoral program for the counseling psychologist is a dissertation. Further, both clinical and counseling graduate students will then compete for the same types of 1-year-long internships.

Remember from Chapter 1 that the APPIC publishes the match rates for students with internship programs. The link, http://www. appic.org/Portals/0/downloads/APPIC_Match_Rates_2011-14_ by_State.pdf, reports a summary of the rates from the years 2011 to 2014. Counseling Ph.D. candidates had a 80% match rate, while clinical Ph.D. candidates had a 79% match rate. Additionally, these matches were typical to APA-accredited internships (91% of the time for clinical and 90% of the time for counseling).

It is also possible to earn a Psy.D. in counseling psychology. I discussed the pros and cons of earning a Psy.D. over a Ph.D. in Chapter 1. We can examine AAPPIC acceptance rates for counseling Ph.D.s and Psy.D.s using the same link as above. Counseling Ph.D. candidates had an 80% match rate and counseling Psy.D. candidates had a 72% match rate. However, of the 80% of Ph.D.s accepted, 90% were matched to an *APA-accredited* site while, of the 72% of Psy.D.s matched, only 45% were matched to an *APA-accredited* site. Again, individual programs will vary widely, so be sure to examine these rates for the schools in which you are interested in attending.

As noted earlier, there are fewer of these programs in existence and, if your desire is to work as a professor at a university, a Psy.D. will not be as advantageous to you, though you will be equally qualified as a Ph.D. for virtually every other job.

Licensing

Again, counseling psychologists undergo the same requirements as clinical psychologists in order to get licensed. Until licensed one cannot see clients without some kind of supervision. Requirements for licensure are the completion of the doctoral program, including the dissertation and the 1-year internship. Then depending on the state, the licensing applicant would need to obtain a prescribed number of supervised client hours. Recall that this means that you are doing therapy but that you confer with a licensed psychologist about the diagnosis, treatment, and progress of your client. Each state has slightly different rules about the amount of these hours needed. Also, in some states, pre-doctoral hours will count as a portion of those supervised hours (i.e., client hours that occurred while you were in school on practicums) as, obviously, will post-doctoral client hours. Once these requirements are met, the licensing candidate can take the EPPP. Each state will dictate what it deems a passing score on this test. This is the identical test taken by clinical psychologists. In fact, a colleague at my university who is a counseling psychologist realized, after noticing that our license numbers were only a couple of digits apart, that we sat for the licensing exam on the same day some 20 years prior. Using the following link, http://c.ymcdn.com/sites/www.asppb.net/resource/resmgr/EPPP_/2012_ASPPB_Exam_Scores_by_Do.pdf, you can see the pass rates for every program in the country. Examine the programs that you are interested in and see how the pass rates compare to those of other schools' programs.

Types of Jobs for which the Degree will Qualify You

A counseling psychologist (with a Ph.D. or Psy.D.) will be qualified for the same types of jobs as a clinical psychologist. Once licensed, insurance companies and agencies view both groups of therapists as "licensed psychologists." Now, based on the philosophy of counseling versus clinical programs (i.e., more wellness, prevention, day-to-day problems versus more serious psychopathology), the two groups may gravitate toward slightly different types of work. Norcross (2000) reports that counseling psychologists are found more often in college counseling centers and clinical psychologists are found more often in hospital and private practice settings. I will now list a few of the places that counseling psychologists may be employed. Notice that in many cases the description is exactly the same as it is in Chapter 1.

College Counseling Center

For a more detailed description and brief history of college counseling centers, please read the College Counseling Center section in Chapter 1. In short, you may know that most every college or university has a counseling center on campus for use by their student population. These centers are often staffed by a combination of professionals and graduate students working toward a degree in psychology, counseling, or social work. These student counselors would be supervised by the professional staff. When I refer students to our counseling center I often explain that fact and then note that this means that they get two counselors for the "price of one." And the price is often free for full-time students at their respective institution.

Some of the common problems seen at college counseling centers include loneliness, body image worries, roommate problems, anxiety, abuse issues, family problems, relationship issues, sexual preference questioning, depression, adjustment to college, achievement issues, and drug and alcohol concerns. The professional staff that are employed in this setting include not just counseling or clinical psychologists but also mental health counselors and social workers.

Inpatient Hospital

Inpatient units in a hospital and/or psychiatric hospital house clients with severe mental health problems who may be a danger to themselves or others. Patients in these facilities may be there voluntarily or involuntarily. Due to insurance restrictions and the theory that patients should be kept in the "least restrictive environment" possible, stays are often not long in an inpatient ward. Among persons with serious mental illness, the average length of hospitalization declined from 12.8 to 9.7 days between 1995 and 2002 (Watanabe-Galloway & Zhang, 2007). Therefore, while individual and group therapy may be part of a psychologist's duties on an inpatient unit, he or she will not engage in long-term therapeutic interventions. A psychologist's goal will be to stabilize and refer the patient to an outpatient agency for follow-up. Psychologists will play an integral role in the evaluation of the patient's status. They will likely be part of a treatment team composed of psychiatrists, social workers, and nurses who work together to design an appropriate treatment plan. Probably the most significant contribution that the psychologist will make on an inpatient unit is his/her skill at assessment. Psychologists will use intelligence and personality testing to help make determinations about an individual's mental state and capabilities.

Many hospitals will also have a partial hospitalization unit that they utilize as a "step down" for patients. Patients come to sessions for several hours a day, several days a week, but live at home. This is more cost-effective and allows the individual to remain at home. Psychologists may be employed doing individual, group, or family therapy on a partial hospitalization unit.

Veterans Administration (VA)

The VA provides inpatient and outpatient facilities for individuals who are or have served in the military. Recall that the VA was instrumental in the creation of counseling psychology. There are still many counseling psychologists who work doing individual, group, and family counseling in their facilities.

Part of a Team at another Type of Facility

Psychologists may also be employed as part of a treatment team at other types of agencies. For example, prisons, group homes, and nursing homes typically have a psychologist on staff. The psychologist will do individual, group, and family therapy and consult with other professionals at the facility to help determine the best treatment plan for individuals in their care.

Outpatient Mental Health Clinic

Many psychologists work in outpatient mental health clinics conducting individual, group, marital, and/or family therapy. Additionally, they may perform psychological assessments using intelligence, personality, and/or aptitude tests and write reports detailing the results.

Private Practice

Many psychologists start their own private practice. While running one's own private practice is often viewed as a career goal, there is a great deal besides doing therapy that goes into it. These practitioners must also be versed in or get assistance in how to choose appropriate office space for a sound price, how to hire (and possibly fire) support staff to answer phones, greet clients, and file insurance claims. For this reason, I often recommend to advisees consider a minor in business while they are an undergraduate. Other psychologists may not own the private practice but work as an independent contractor in someone else's practice. In that capacity they hold no responsibility for the business side of the practice but see clients for therapy or assessment. They are typically paid a percentage of what the practice owner receives from insurance and/or client payments.

University Professor

With a Ph.D. in counseling psychology, one can also gain employment at a university as a professor. Recall from the section on employment in Chapter 1 that if you have earned a Psy.D. in counseling psychology, this type of job will not typically be an option, as most universities will require a Ph.D. (which requires the conducting of original research) for consideration of a tenure-track position. Professors will obviously teach classes in their respective area, but they will also engage in conducting research. Work at a university will also usually involve being a part of the university community by serving on committees. The salary will often be less than that of a counseling psychologist who works in a clinical position. However, there are other perks, such as not teaching in the summer or having good insurance and retirement benefits that often make up for the lower salary.

Earning Potential

As has been noted, there are a great deal of similarities between clinical and counseling psychologists. This is true for salary as well. In fact the *Occupational Outlook Handbook* groups the two professions together when reporting the typical earnings of individuals in these professions. Actually, a more significant determinate for salary than whether one is a counseling or clinical psychologist is in the type of institution where one is employed. According to the *Handbook*, the median pay for both counseling and clinical psychologists in 2012 was $67,280.

References

Altmaier, E. M., & Hansen, J. C. (Eds.) (2011). *The Oxford handbook of counseling psychology*. New York: Oxford University Press.

Meara, N. M., & Myers, R. A. (1999). A history of Division 17 (Counseling Psychology): Establishing stability amid change. In D. A.Dewsbury (Ed.), *Unification through division: Histories of the divisions of the American Psychological Association*, *Vol. 3* (pp. 9–41). Washington, DC: American Psychological Association.

Munley, P. H., Duncan L. E., McDonnell, K. A., & Sauer, E. M. (2004). Counseling psychology in the United States of America. *Counselling Psychology Quarterly*, 17(3), 247–271.

Norcross, J. C. (2000). Clinical v. counseling psychology: What's the diff? *Eye on Psi Chi*, 5(1), 20–22.

Occupational outlook handbook (2014–15 ed.). Washington, DC: Bureau of Labor Statistics, U.S. Department of Labor.

Rude, S. S., Weissberg, M. G., & Gazda, G. M. (1988). Looking to the future: Themes from the third national conference for counseling psychology. *The Counseling Psychologist*, 16(3), 423–430.

Super, D. E. (1955). Transition: From vocational guidance to counseling psychology. *Journal of Counseling Psychology*, 2, 3–9.

Vera, E. (2012). *The Oxford handbook of prevention in counseling psychology*. New York: Oxford University Press.

Watanabe-Galloway, S., & Zhang, W. (2007). Analysis of US trends in discharges from general hospitals for episodes of serious mental illness, 1995–2002. Psychiatric Services, 58(4), 496–502.

3

Master's in Social Work (MSW)

Overall History and Philosophy of the Profession

The oldest mental health profession is social work. Its beginning can be traced back to the mid-1800s and the end of the Civil War. Glicken (2011) points out that the economic depression and racism, coupled with the rapid influx of immigrants, created a need for social programs and social agencies to assist citizens with the financial and social hardships of the time. Specifically, poverty was one of the major social problems. The "helping" of those who were struggling involved a two-pronged approach. First, there was the more individual assistance offered in the way of financial, housing, and affiliation. Second, those in the profession knew that, to really help an individual, societal changes were also necessary. So the philosophy of social work can be thought of as broader than that of other professions; that is, individual assistance coupled with actively bringing about broad social and/or societal changes.

The work done with the individual began to be known as casework. Casework eventually became more specialized and could be thought of as medical, psychiatric, and child casework. One early organization known for its casework with the individual was the Charity Organization Society (COS). In 1897 the COS in New York partnered with Columbia University and developed the first formal training program in social work. By 1919 there were 17 schools of social work. They formed a

Careers in Mental Health: Opportunities in Psychology, Counseling, and Social Work,
First Edition. Kim Metz.
© 2016 John Wiley & Sons, Ltd. Published 2016 by John Wiley & Sons, Ltd.

professional organization entitled the Association of Training Schools of Professional Social Work. This organization is the precursor of today's Council of Social Work Education (CSWE).

World War I brought further growth in social work, just as it had done for psychiatrists and psychologists. Social workers expanded their work with poverty-related issues to now include work with soldiers returning from war. The trauma those soldiers experienced often led to them experiencing problems adjusting at home. The term "shell-shocked" was used to describe the affected soldiers, though we would now attribute their difficulties to symptoms of post-traumatic stress syndrome (PTSD). Because it was believed that family assistance was necessary to help the troubled soldiers, work with these soldiers often included their family and finding ways that they could best assist their loved one. By 1927 social workers were employed at over 100 guidance clinics working with middle-class clients who had experienced war trauma (Tannenbaum & Reisch, 2001). Typically, they worked on teams with psychiatrists and psychologists to aid the soldiers and their families.

The next major historical event to influence social work was the Great Depression. The stock market crash in 1929 led to the loss of life savings of many families and the closing of numerous businesses. Unemployment skyrocketed until the unemployment rate topped 25%. Americans' view of poverty began to change in that they felt those who were struggling were doing so, not due to personal failings but because of the dire financial circumstances of the country (Tannenbaum & Reisch, 2001). In an effort to combat the growing poverty, in 1933 President Roosevelt introduced the New Deal. This program increased government control and regulation of many businesses in an effort to ensure their stability – the idea being that Americans needed government assistance to maximize their quality of life.

A central part of this program was the beginning of the Social Security program (Tannenbaum & Reisch, 2001) in which the government saved a portion of a wage earner's paycheck for later in life when they retired. The government was not confident that its citizens would be able to do so on their own. This is just one example of the many new government programs that were put in place following the Depression. These hosts of programs were the precursor to our current social welfare system. Additionally, these programs, which needed personnel to manage and implement them, expanded the role and visibility of social workers. In the 1930s and 1940s the number of social workers in the United States increased from 40,000 to 80,000 (Glicken, 2011).

Then, as World War II was occurring, social workers found themselves in even more demand. They were called upon to help soldiers and their families cope with the emotional aftermath of war as well as with the financial/employment difficulties that existed in their families and communities. With the increase in the number of social workers and the recent increase in the number of social service agencies, there was a movement to standardize training programs and raise the educational component of them (Glicken, 2011). This movement led to the formation of the CSWE in 1952. Further, the National Association of Social Workers was founded in 1955.

While the number of social service programs were increasing in the 1940s and 1950s, many of those programs were instituted in order to serve middle-class white citizens instead of primarily the poor, as had been the emphasis in the past (Glicken, 2011). During this time a more negative attitude about the poor and those in poverty was cultivated, and there was less social activism in the United States. This partially occurred because of the economic upturn that followed the end of World War II. Couple this with the return home of soldiers who were ready to not only be employed but also buy a plethora of things from cars to homes to housewares, and you have an increase in prosperity. These soldiers also started families that resulted in the "baby boom," which led to more demand for products and merchandise. One commentator described post-war America as an "affluent society," noting that, "in the old world, poverty was an all-pervasive fact of life, but that in the contemporary United States, social and economic policies should be based on the fact that the ordinary individual has access to amenities – foods, entertainment, personal transportation, and plumbing – in which not even the rich rejoiced a century ago" (Galbraith, 1984).

So, to review, in the 1920s and 1930s people who were struggling financially were seen as unfortunate and as needing assistance from the government and/or others. Then by the 1940s and 1950s, Americans believed that citizens needed to "pull themselves up by their boot-straps" and work harder to achieve more prosperity rather than rely on the government or others for assistance. The pendulum shifted again in the 1960s. Social critic Michael Harrington emphasized what he termed the "Other America" and those Americans who seem to have been bypassed in the country's climb to more prosperity. He noted that 40–50 million people were working menial and/or sporadic jobs and not enjoying the perks of the so-called "affluent society." Indeed, Martin Luther King, Jr. used the poverty of the "Other America" to explain the cause of the Watts riots that occurred in Los Angeles in 1965. He stated, "I would minimize the racial significance [of the riots] and point to the fact that these were the rumblings of discontent from the 'have-nots' within the midst of an affluent society" (see Carson, 1998, pp. 291–292).

Due to this shift in the views of poverty and the poor, a new array of government programs were implemented. Specifically, the Economic Opportunity Act (EOC) of 1964 sparked the beginning of programs such as Job Corps, Upward Bound, Community Action, and Head Start. In addition, the Department of Housing and Urban Development (HUD), Medicare and Medicaid, and the Food Stamp program were established. In turn, these new programs and agencies led to more jobs and greater visibility for social workers.

As should be expected, as time marched on the pendulum swung again. In the mid- to late 1970s many Americans, including those getting assistance, were becoming unhappy with the number of government programs and subsequently the amount of government involvement in their lives (Glicken, 2011). Additionally, Americans were looking for ways to reduce taxes. Further, Ronald Reagan, a more conservative president, was now in office. As a result of these social and political influences, many of the social service programs were cut, provided less funding or were turned over to private-sector agencies to manage. This impacted the role of social workers as the cutbacks came at a time when the country was struggling with the spread of AIDS and the rampant abuse of crack cocaine. Additionally, at that time issues such as homelessness and domestic violence were getting increased attention. The role of social workers changed from not just being frontline workers but to managing new public-run agencies and becoming advocates for social reforms for the disadvantaged (Glicken, 2011). The push away from assistance to the poor continued into the Clinton administration, when it was clear that Americans were concerned about "welfare dependence" in which people may choose to not work in order to collect benefits. Therefore, after the passage of the Welfare Reform Bill in 1996, limits to the welfare program were established.

Other changes in the social work profession at this time included a raised awareness of diversity, which led to efforts to increase diversity (in both race and gender) in the profession and in the role of diversity in the course content of graduate schools. Additionally, the Bachelor's in Social Work (BSW) became the industry standard. Further, social workers began to work in private. You will see in the next section that the work involving clients in a private practice setting, that is conducting therapy, is separate and distinct from the direct service or more hands-on work involving matching clients with appropriate services, which had been the mainstay of social workers until that time.

Three other influences during this time period impacted the profession (Tannenbaum & Reisch, 2001). First, there was increased pressure to move the bulk of casework or social work from state and federal governmental agencies to private nonprofit agencies. Second, the beginning of "managed care" in the United States had an impact on not only the administration of medical health care but also on mental health care. Managed care required alterations in the practice of social workers, as well as other mental health professionals, largely because managed care meant that an outside entity had some control of the types and amount of medical and mental health care for which a professional could be reimbursed (Cohen, 2003). A third influence on the profession was that diversity became more central to the teaching of social work. In fact, the CSWE modified the program requirements of graduate programs to include coursework that encouraged and instructed students to work for social justice.

In the last two decades there continue to be social problems. For example, in the financial arena there have been problems with funding both Medicare and Social Security, issues that directly affect not only the poor but all Americans. Further, the recession in the mid-2000s drastically impacted the savings of many Americans. Additionally, the bursting of the housing bubble and the banking crisis in the late 2000s have also crippled some Americans financially.

Our current issues are not only related to finances, we also continue to struggle with issues such as crime, education, and the changing make-up of the family. These are issues that social workers will continue to attempt to manage and ameliorate along with our political leaders and educators.

Education

The type of education needed in order to be a social worker really depends upon the type of social worker one would like to be. There are actually three broad types of social workers (and as you will see soon, some more specific specializations). One can become a macro social worker, a direct service social worker, or a clinical social worker. I have, therefore, divided up this section based on these various options available to students in the social work arena.

Macro Social Worker

A *macro social worker* will be employed at the community or societal level. He or she may manage institutions that assist people, be instrumental in developing or examining public policy, or design programs to meet the needs of a community. In their textbook about macro social work, Netting, Kettner, McMurtry, and Thomas (2012) define macro practice as "professionally guided intervention(s) designed to bring about change in organizational, community, and/or policy arenas." For example, a macro social worker may try to inform politicians about public policy related to human service by being a lobbyist. Further, a macro social worker may try to increase public awareness of an issue, such as bullying or the incarceration of juveniles, in order to help institute positive change in the area by perhaps proposing a program to assist with the community issue. If this sounds interesting to you, then a master's degree in macro social work may be something to research further.

Given that you are reading this text, you are probably more interested in the next two types of social workers: the direct service social worker and the clinical social worker. The terms are somewhat confusing because both actually provide direct service (versus the macro social worker who indirectly affects citizens) but they do so in different ways and the educational degree needed for each is different.

Direct Service Social Worker

The *direct service social worker* typically requires only an undergraduate or bachelor's degree in social work. Not every college has social work as a major so if you choose this option, be selective in the colleges to which you apply to ensure that they offer an undergraduate degree in social work. Just like with every other profession discussed in these pages, it is essential that the program be accredited by the profession's accrediting body in order to ensure that it is meeting basic requirements and standards for training in the area. In this case, the program you choose should be accredited by the CSWE.

It should be noted that, of all the mental health professions that have been discussed, social work is the only one that has the profession's accrediting body monitor and accredit its bachelor's level programs. Most accrediting bodies in mental health do not accredit educational programs until the master's level. There are two other things that make a bachelor's in social work more unique than the other bachelor's level majors with a human service emphasis, such as psychology or sociology. First, as you will see, the social work profession has a licensing process for its bachelor's level graduates. Most mental health professions cannot earn a license until they have received at least their master's degree. In the case of psychology, practitioners cannot be licensed until they have received a doctoral degree. A second unique thing about social work undergraduate programs is that, while some psychology and other human service undergraduate majors may offer an internship opportunity, only the undergraduate social work program requires that students complete an internship.

The job of a direct service social worker is typically to match up clients and appropriate services. Direct service social workers may do initial screenings or intakes of clients, and they may help determine whether individuals meet criteria for specific programs or services. Direct service social workers cannot conduct psychotherapy. They may engage in a form of counseling, but keep in mind that the term "counseling" is a loose term. The definition of counseling is to guide or to advise. That is not the same thing as conducting psychotherapy, which can be defined as "the informed and intentional application of clinical methods and interpersonal stances derived from established psychological principles for the purpose of assisting people to modify

their behaviors, cognitions, emotions, and/or other personal characteristics in directions that the participants deem desirable" (Norcross,
1990, pp. 218–220). Therefore, while direct service social work may
seem advantageous because it requires less education, you are also
limited in the types of jobs or job duties in which you may engage.
Some may choose to earn their bachelor's degree in social work
and then work in the field while they continue their education in a
master's program.

Clinical Social Worker

A *clinical social worker* typically conducts the traditional type of face-
to-face counseling or mental health therapy that most readers of this
text are likely to be interested in pursuing. Many clinical social workers
are employed in a mental health center or are part of a private practice
and do individual or family or marital counseling. In order to work as
a clinical social worker, an individual would need a master's degree in
social work. Just as with the undergraduate degree programs mentioned above, one should be sure to enroll in programs that are
accredited by the CSWE.

It should be noted that, while many students may enter a master's
program after earning a bachelor's degree in social work, it is not
necessary for your bachelor's degree to be in social work. An undergraduate degree in virtually any area is acceptable. Having said that,
most students will have likely majored in some type of human service
major, such as psychology or sociology. A master's program will typically take about two years to complete, although some programs run
through summers and may, therefore, allow for graduation in about
16 months. Further, if your undergraduate degree was in social work,
you may have to take less coursework than those with degrees in other
fields. This greatly depends on each individual university and program,
so be sure to research the types of programs in which you have the
most interest. Foundational classes that are often required in many
master's social work programs include courses such as Human Behavior
and Social Environment, Fundamentals of Social Work Research,
Social Welfare, Social Work Policy, and Social Work Practice.
Additionally, courses such as Social Work Practice with Children and
Adolescents or Social Work with Older Populations or Family Therapy
Practice or Death and Grief, among many others, may be offered.

Beyond the core of courses that may be required, a student will also engage in a set number of practicum hours in which he or she will get experience working in community settings and practicing social work under supervision. Following completion of a master's in social work program, as with the other helping professions, a student will also need to obtain a license to practice in the field.

Licensing

Licensing involves earning a set score on an exam as well as gaining supervised experience in the field. Licensing exams for social workers are administered by the American Social Worker Board (ASWB). All 50 states use the same exams. The board actually offers four types of exams: Bachelor's, Master's, Advanced Generalist, and Clinical. However, not every state requires every exam. The website http://www.socialworklicensure.org/ allows you to choose your state and examine the licensing requirements for each category or level of social worker.

Therefore, it is possible that, if you plan to obtain only a bachelor's degree in social work and hope to be employed as a direct service social worker, you may still need to take a licensing exam, one designed for bachelor-level students. On the other hand, in some states the exam will not be necessary at that level.

Licensing is definitely required for clinical social workers in all states. Once again, the exact requirements for licensure vary from state the state. Again, utilize the http://www.socialworklicensure.org/ website and/or do a search for your own state's licensing board for specifics. There are some generalities for clinical social workers. First, students need to possess a master's degree in social work. Second, the exam for master's level students must be passed. The exam contains 170 questions, only 150 of which are scored. The other 20 are used as pre-test questions for possible inclusion on a future exam. The test is administered electronically, and test takers are given four hours to complete it.

Finally, in addition to passing the exam, clinical social work licensure candidates will have to obtain the state-required number of supervised hours before they can earn their license. Supervised hours refer to hours spent seeing clients whom you will later discuss with your supervisor, a licensed social worker. During supervision meetings, which are often held on a weekly basis, the diagnosis, treatment, and progress of your clients will be discussed. States will vary on the amount of super-vised experience needed to qualify for a license.

   At this point it is instructive to note that, just as licensing require-ments vary slightly from state to state, so do the titles given to professionals in the area. For example, Licensed Social Worker (LSW) does not mean the same thing in every state. In some states LSW signifies a bachelor's prepared professional, and in some states it is the title for a master's prepared professional. When people reach the highest level of practice, their title typically contains words such as "independent," "clinical," or "independent clinical." The abbrevia-tions used could then be LISW, LCSW or LICSW, respectively. This once again illustrates the necessity of checking your own state's licensing requirements.

Types of Jobs for which the Degree will Qualify You

Macro Social Worker

Administrator of a social service agency This can include myriad possibilities. One could be employed as the director of a nonprofit agency or a mental health organization. One could also work in the administration of a government agency that specializes in social service. Additionally, macro social workers may lobby for societal changes within the city or state in which they reside. Moreover, a macro social worker will be attempting to make changes at the organization level, the community level, or even the national level. For example, a macro social worker could be employed at a university counseling center trying to implement programs that may help the college community. In that example, one could perhaps design a program to help reduce violence on campus or to assist freshmen with the transition to college.

Researcher Many macro-level social workers aspire to conduct research in a particular area. This is most often accomplished at a university by a social worker who is also a faculty member who engages in research. Recall that a doctoral degree is typically required of faculty members at most colleges and universities. There are also research institutes that examine social problems and mental health issues. Again, an advanced degree is often necessary as knowledge of experimental methods and statistics, which is a significant part of doctoral curricula, is crucial to be an effective researcher. Finally, national, state, and local governments sometimes have a need for someone to research a particular social problem in their respective community in order to determine the exact nature of and solution to the problem.

Direct Service Social Worker

Many of the positions listed here will only require a bachelor's degree. However, laws in your state and the requirements of an individual agency may change that. Be aware that these positions will typically pay less than either the macro social worker or the clinical social worker since less education is required. There is also high turnover in these jobs as, in addition to the low pay rate, they can be stressful. Social workers may be employed in some of the following positions while they pursue a master's degree. Also remember that, with only a bachelor's degree, one will not be doing therapy with clients. However, there is a great deal of opportunity to counsel and advise and make an immediate difference in the life of a troubled child or adult. Note that these are also positions for which many bachelor-level *psychology or sociology* graduates may be qualified.

Public welfare This would involve work at agencies such as the Bureau of Disability or Human Services. Overall, work involves helping the elderly, the sick, the disabled, or the poor. Responsibilities could include case management, policy setting, or administrative duties.

Child welfare Employment in this area involves ensuring the safety and well-being of children and adolescents. This would include work in governmental agencies such as children's service agencies (known variously as Children's Service, the Department of Family Services, or a similar title depending on your locality). Job responsibilities at such an agency might include doing evaluations regarding child abuse and/ or neglect or conducting case management of identified clients or assisting with remediation for a family once they have become active in the system. One could also engage in case management, advocacy, or intervention at adoption agencies or foster care agencies.

Hospitals   According to the *Occupation Outlook Handbook* compiled by the Bureau of Labor Statistics one-third of direct service social workers are employed in a hospital setting where they focus on maintaining the medical and emotional health of a patient. These professionals are often referred to as medical social workers or health care social workers. They attempt to help patients understand their diagnosis and they assist in making appropriate decisions regarding the patient's housing, work, or lifestyle issues. For example, they can be involved in the case management of patients after a hospital stay – helping to determine whether it is safe or manageable to return home after their stay or if they need an alternative placement. Work in this area requires not only good communication skills with the patient but also with their family. Additionally, a medical social worker must be versed in rules and policies of a variety of insurance companies in order to make the best determination of realistic options for any given patient.

Other medically driven agencies   Direct service social workers might also work in public health programs, the VA, nursing homes, or hospices. Again, counseling with family members and loved ones will be central to their duties. For example, the goal of a hospice is to help clients and their families adapt to terminal illness. Hospices provide what's called palliative care, which means that their job is to make the patient as comfortable and dignified as possible as they endure their illness. This includes physical pain management but also includes helping them manage their day-to-day living. Hospice care often takes place in a patient's own home. Therefore, social workers might arrange for in-home nursing care for a patient or for equipment to be delivered that will assist with care of the patient. Alternatively, there are also now freestanding, in-patient hospice facilities and/or sometimes hospice care will be delivered on a particular floor or wing of a hospital. These are also environments in which a social worker might be employed. Similarly, a social worker might be employed at a nursing home helping to maintain or increase the quality of life of its clients. A social worker at a VA would do similar activities but be working with men and women who served in the military. There are both inpatient and outpatient VA facilities.

Criminal justice or correctional facilities   Social workers may be employed in jails, prisons, or other correctional facilities. Mental health workers in the criminal justice system are focused on rehabilitation of their clients. Their duties could include some type of counseling and/or group work with the inmates. They may also be involved in facilitating day-to-day activities within the facility. In addition to correctional facilities, social workers may be work for the courts, as probation or parole officers, or as victim advocates.

School social work   Some schools may make use of social workers to assist students with emotional, behavioral, or academic problems. They may involve the family or teachers in their interventions. Additionally, they may work with problems such as truancy or bullying. These types of positions may be filled by a social worker or by a school counselor or school psychologist. Each school district will make decisions regarding educational background and experience of someone with this position. Those decisions are often influenced by the amount of money a district possesses, as educational positions will likely be funded first.

Clinical Social Worker

Clinical social workers will hold a master's degree in social work. They will diagnose and treat emotional, mental, and behavioral disorders.

Mental health agency   Clinical social workers can be employed at community mental health agencies as clinicians who conduct individual, family, and/or group therapy. At a mental health agency, a job responsibility of a social worker may also be raising awareness of specific issues to the public. For example, he or she may organize a workshop for parents of toddlers in which they discuss various parenting techniques or may educate high school teachers in a workshop about self-mutilating behaviors in adolescents.

Private practice   Clinical social workers might also work at a private practice. This can be a practice that they own and run or one that is owned by someone else in which they practice as an independent contractor. Recall from Chapter 1 that an independent contractor conducts therapy with clients and receives a percentage of the money that the practice earns from either the client or the insurance company. The advantage is that one does not have responsibility for the business side of the practice (e.g., hiring or firing therapists or support staff, filing insurance claims, finding and affording office space). If you choose to run a practice you will engage in those activities, however, you will also be earning money from the labors of the therapists who work for you. It is very much a business venture, so if this is an aspiration, consider a business minor during your undergraduate years. As an independent contractor in a private practice, one could see a variety of clients for individual, group, or marital counseling. The area in which you spend most of your time practicing will partially depend on the emphasis of the program from which you graduated. That is, you would practice within your area of expertise – seeing the types of clients and utilizing the therapy modality for which you have been trained.

College counseling centers   As discussed in Chapter 1, licensed social workers may be employed at college counseling centers serving students who attend that particular university.

Other agencies

Most of the agencies discussed in the preceding section on direct service social workers may also employ (and sometimes prefer) master's trained social workers. So employment in welfare agencies, hospitals or other medical institutions, correctional facilities, or schools may also be job options. As a master's prepared clinician, earning potential will typically be higher than bachelor's prepared counterparts.

Earning Potential

Obviously, earning potential will depend to a great degree on the part of the country in which you reside, on the type of education level you achieve, and on the type of agency in which you are employed. First, I will give you some generalities about social work compensation. According to the *Occupational Outlook Handbook* the median pay for a social worker in 2012 was $44,200. Unfortunately, the *Handbook* does not distinguish between those social workers with bachelor's degrees and those with master's degrees. It does note that the pay of the lowest 10 % of social workers is $27,450 and the pay of the top 10% of earners is $72,980. It is a good guess that the lower-paying jobs belong to entry-level bachelor trained social workers and the highest-paying jobs are held by more seasoned master's level trained social workers. The *Handbook* further points out the types of industries that seem to pay social workers the highest amount. That is, social workers employed in hospitals typically earned more ($56,290) than those in schools ($54,590), who typically earned more than those working in governmental agencies ($44,370.) The lower-paying agencies, in general, tend to be nursing and residential care facilities ($34,950) and social service agencies ($37,170).

References

Carson, C. (Ed.). (1998). *The autobiography of Martin Luther King, Jr.* New York: Time Warner.

Cohen, J. (2003). Managed care and the evolving role of the clinical social worker in mental health. *Social Work*, 48(1), 34–43.

Galbraith, J. K. (1984). *The affluent society.* Boston: Houghton Mifflin.

Glicken, M. D. (2011). *Social work in the 21st century: An introduction to social welfare, social issues, and the profession.* Phoenix, AZ: Sage.

Netting, E., Kettner, P., McMurtry, M., & Thomas, M. (2012). *Social work macro practice.* New York: Pearson.

Norcross, J. C. (1990). An eclectic definition of psychotherapy. In J. K. Zeig & W. M. Munion (Eds.), *What is psychotherapy? Contemporary perspectives* (pp. 218–220). San Francisco, CA: Jossey-Bass.

Occupational outlook handbook (2014–15 ed.). Washington, DC: Bureau of Labor Statistics, U.S. Department of Labor.

Tannenbaum, N., & Reisch, M. (2001). Charitable volunteers to architects of social welfare: A brief history of social work. *Ongoing Magazine*, Fall, 7–12.

4

Master's in Counseling

Overall History and Philosophy of the Profession

Mental health counseling has a briefer history than psychology or social work. Many label it as one of the youngest mental health professions. While counselors have been practicing since World War II and have their roots in the same economic and historical events as psychologists and social workers, they have only more recently became organized and developed a route for licensure and credentialing. In this section, I will delineate some of the most significant historical events that helped shaped the counseling profession. Keep in mind that this profession of mental health counseling (in which you can become licensed with a master's degree) is distinct from counseling psychology (which requires a Ph.D. for licensure), despite the similarities in their names and the amount of history that they share.

As stated, the roots of mental health counseling date back to events mentioned in the history of psychology and social work. Specifically, events that were related to vocational counseling had the biggest influence on the counseling profession. Thus, recall that in the late 1800s the Industrial Revolution necessitated an increased number of personnel to help citizens find vocations that they were best suited for and that would enable them to support their families. Recall also that Frank Parsons opened the Vocation Bureau in Boston to assist people

Careers in Mental Health: Opportunities in Psychology, Counseling, and Social Work,
First Edition. Kim Metz.
© 2016 John Wiley & Sons, Ltd. Published 2016 by John Wiley & Sons, Ltd.

in finding careers appropriate to their skills and personality. Then Clifford Beers wrote his influential book detailing the deplorable conditions within inpatient hospitals in the late 1800s and early 1900s. His work shed more light on mental illness and its treatment and led to reforms in the system. Significantly, the reforms enabled him to establish the first mental health clinic in America, which would later be a place for counselors to be employed.

Given the increased attention to the vocational issues of Americans, in 1910 the National Vocational Guidance Association (NVGA) was founded. It united individuals who had an interest in vocational counseling. This organization can be considered a precursor to today's American Counseling Association. Then, in 1917, the Smith–Hughes Act was passed, which provided funds to schools to conduct vocational education with students. Soon after this, as you know from previous chapters, World War I and later World War II necessitated that more money and energy be devoted to the training and placement of soldiers before their service began. Those resources were further utilized when the soldiers returned home in order to help them find suitable jobs/careers, given their skills and preferences.

The 1920s saw the development of standards that were used to evaluate the usefulness and validity of new psychometric tests. This led to the publication of new psychological measures, including the Strong Interest Inventory in 1927, which could be used to measure an individual's interests and assist him/her in seeing how those interests might influence an appropriate career choice. While this solidified the counselor's role of vocational counselor, two other events expanded the role significantly. First, the publication of John Brewer's work in 1932 and second the publication of Rogers' book in 1942.

Brewer published *Education as Guidance* in 1932 and in it he proposed that the vocational choices of students should not be the sole emphasis of guidance personnel. He actually advocated for teachers to be counselors, in that they should equip students with the problem-solving and decision-making skills and knowledge base that would enable them to make their own informed choices about their future careers. Further, he felt that education should seek to prepare students for any inevitable issues related to living and that curricula should incorporate guidance into the classroom (Gysbers, 2001). Counselors began to see their role expanding beyond vocational counselor and moving more toward personal counselor. They now viewed a larger part of their responsibility to be assisting students with problems in living beyond career choice issues. Then, in the 1940s, Carl Rogers published an influential book titled *Counseling and Psychotherapy*. In his book, Rogers challenged the notion that the therapist or counselor was the "expert" and instead theorized that the therapeutic relationship should be more client-centered. That is, the counselor or therapist is not "in charge" but is working with clients to assist them to uncover what helps them the most. His approach was termed "nondirective" and was considered a psychological approach to therapy in contrast with Freud's psychoanalysis and with behavioral and cognitive theories. We know it now as a humanistic approach. Rogers had ardent advocates as well as harsh critics. What he did for the profession of counseling, though, broadened it even more. Instead of focusing only on vocations, these professionals began to look at the importance of other aspects of a client's life. In fact, Gladding (2012) notes that "guidance for all intents and purposes suddenly disappeared as a major consideration in the bulk of the literature and was replaced by a decade or more of consideration on counseling."

Several occurrences in the 1950s contributed further to the evolution of counseling. Many of these concerned the gathering of like-minded individuals into organizations. In general, once established, a professional *group* is able to garner more support and visibility than disconnected *individuals*. Moreover, the group is able to further define the goals and training needed in a profession. Groups such as the American Personnel and Guidance Association (APGA) and the American School Counselor Association (ASCA) were formed in 1952 and 1953, respectively. Additionally, remember that Division 17 of the APA was formed in 1946. It was known as the Division of Counseling Psychology. Notably, the division was previously referred to as the Division of Counseling and Guidance, but the words "and Guidance" were dropped from its name before attaching itself to the APA. Counseling psychology remains separate from mental health counseling, and the shift in the nomenclature of the APA had an impact on the profession of counseling in general. Recall also that the VA was looking for professionals to counsel veterans and that there simply were not enough clinical psychologists. Therefore, this was one reason for the new Division. The other was that the profession hoped to distinguish itself from clinical psychology. Once formed, the Division was more able to define itself. For example, Super (1955) indicated that counseling psychology was more concerned with normal human development than severe psychopathology, and that it was influenced by vocational counseling and the humanistic approach to psychotherapy. In this way counseling (either counseling psychology or, soon, mental health counseling) set itself apart from its clinical counterparts.

In the 1960s there were societal influences that began to shape the field of counseling. According to Gladding (2012), the impact of the developmental model began to fade in favor of helping people find ways to cope with three major events: the Vietnam War, the Civil Rights Movement, and the Women's Movement. Counselors were looking for ways to help people cope with the societal and personal tensions that resulted from these events. In 1963 the passage of the Community Mental Health Centers Act led to the creation of mental health centers. The passage of this act was largely achieved because there was a push to have people treated in less constrained environments than inpatient hospitals. For example, President Kennedy urged the mental health community to get "patients out of mental institutions and back into their homes and communities" (Dworkin, 2012). This meant that the role of counselors was expanded beyond the educational setting. Additionally, as you can imagine, it opened up new job opportunities for counselors (as well as psychologists and social workers).

Many counselors were still being trained in departments of education. Training had historically focused on vocational counseling and had first been expanded to include training in normal development and then to how to help individuals cope with adverse environmental and societal events. However, their training was not specifically in social work, psychology, or medicine so while they at times performed job functions similar to their mental health counterparts, the counselors lacked a professional organization and did not possess credentials that would enable them to become licensed (Pistole, 2001). Therefore, in the early 1970s a grassroots movement began to organize themselves into a professional organization that could help refine their identity in the mix of mental health professionals.

In July 1978 the American Mental Health Counselors Association (AMHCA) was formed. It helped counselors solidify their identity and clarify their goals and roles (Gladding, 2012). Pistole (2001) describes the counselor profession as one that "endorses a philosophy that is focused more on strengths and wellness, as springing from the multiple synthesized domains of the person, and focused less on curing some kind of mental illness." Further, she asserts that as health care and managed care have evolved, so has the work of the mental health counselor. Therefore, she indicates that "remedial intervention as well as the diagnosis and treatment of psychopathology has been synthesized within the mental health counselor's underlying philosophy of strengthening and restoring development and mental health."

The other significant advance for the profession in the 1970s was related to licensure. Gladding (2012) notes that at that time the APA began to set stricter limits on who could take its licensing exam. For example, it did not allow students who graduated from education departments to sit for the exam. This was obviously a stumbling block for many counselors and it led the APGA to advocate for its own state licensing laws. Virginia was the first to do so in 1976. Most others followed suit throughout the 1980s and 1990s. In 2007 and 2010, Nevada and California, respectively, were the last states to develop rules to regulate counselors.

In the 1980s the counseling profession became more solid with the development of the Council for Accreditation of Counseling & Related Educational Programs (CACREP). Its role was to refine training requirements and accredit counseling programs to ensure that they were meeting basic standards. This increased the credibility and identity of this relatively newly defined profession. CACREP accredits master and doctoral programs. There are several types of programs eligible for accreditation and they will each be discussed in the Education section.

To further clarify the profession of counseling, the APGA made a decision to change its name. Recall that APGA stands for the American Personnel and Guidance Association and it was significant in helping to define the profession of counseling. However, in the 1980s, it became clear that "personnel" and "guidance" were no longer as illustrative of the profession. This professional association changed its name to the American Association for Counseling and Development (AACD).

As you can see, counseling is one of the youngest human service professions (Pistole, 2001). While the roots of the counseling profession span back to the 1950s and even earlier, it has really only been since the early 1980s that counselors have begun to define themselves as a unique mental health profession.

Education

In order to work as a mental health counselor, one must obtain a master's degree in mental health counseling. When considering graduate programs in counseling (or marriage and family therapy, as we will discuss in the next chapter), it is very important that students ensure that the program is accredited by the CACREP. As discussed above, this body exists in order to evaluate and critique counseling programs to ensure that they are meeting basic standards within their curriculum. At the CACREP website, http://www.cacrep.org/directory/, you can do a search for schools in a particular geographical area that have CACREP-accredited programs. The training specified by the CACREP includes 60 credit hours of coursework and supervised clinical experience.

Programs that offer a master's in counseling typically offer it in one or more areas of counseling. So your master's degree would be in one of these categories or specializations. Currently, CACREP accredits master's degrees in six areas of counseling, which will be described below. Please note that some of these programs are more common than others. After a brief description of each, I will list the number of universities that offer such a program. Realize also that many of these specialties seem to be closely related to degrees in other programs. For example, you can get a master's degree from a counseling program where your specialization is marriage, couple and family counseling or you can get a master's degree in marriage and family therapy (discussed in Chapter 5). *Yes, it is confusing.*

Following is a list of types of accredited counseling programs, which was garnered from the CACREP website. Before examining each program it should be noted that the CACREP standards underwent an overhaul in 2009. Some program titles were dropped and/or modified. Therefore, if the program, which is typically accredited for 10 years at a time, was in the middle of its accreditation cycle it likely retains its original name as of now. When those programs come up for review those program titles will be dropped. For example, the Student Affairs and College Counseling program is one of which the title has recently been modified. Therefore, you may still find programs under the old names, for example, College Counseling, Student Affairs or Student Affairs and College Counseling. Further, there are Community Counseling programs, which you will not see listed below. That is due to the fact that programs with that title will be subsumed under the Community Mental Health Counseling title when they come up for reaccreditation. Following, please find a list of the current specializations that may be offered at various programs. If you decide to go the route of mental health counselor in order to fulfill your dream of helping people, please think carefully about which area you would most like to specialize in. Further, you may find programs that offer more than one specialization. If time permits, consider opting to do coursework in both specializations. This could be advantageous; first, to increase your marketability and second, to increase your longevity in the mental health arena as you may decide to switch emphases later in your career.

Clinical Mental Health Counseling

Students learn to work with clients who are experiencing emotional and mental disorders. Students are also trained to promote mental health and wellness. These counselors can see clients individually, as a family, or in groups. They will learn to diagnose, treat, and prevent mental health problems. They may be employed as part of an interdisciplinary team or work in private practice, community mental health centers, hospitals, or other treatment centers. After School Counseling (discussed next), this is the most common master's program offered. There are 149 CACREP-accredited programs in the United States. An additional 86 programs are titled Community Counseling but, as noted, will undergo a name change when they are reaccredited.

School Counseling

Students in this program area will train to work with K-12 students in school settings. Graduate students will be trained to promote the academic, the career, and the personal and social development of the student with whom they work. Eventual job responsibilities include individual counseling, group counseling, classroom guidance, and consultation with family and teachers regarding student needs. There are 239 School Counseling programs in the United States. If this is an area in which you are interested in studying, be sure to also examine Chapter 7 (School Psychology), as that profession also works with children and adolescents in schools. I will try to distinguish between these two possibilities (school counselor and school psychologist) in Chapter 7.

Addiction Counseling

Students are trained to work with individuals and/or families who are experiencing difficulty related to the abuse of alcohol, drugs, gambling, sex, and other addictive disorders. Once licensed, a graduate might work in private practice or in a community mental health center or in some type of community agency that specializes in substance abuse services, such as an inpatient treatment center. There are only three programs in the United States that offer this type of master's in counseling programs. As you will see in Chapter 6, there are other types of programs that will enable you to work with individuals with chemical dependency or substance abuse problems.

Career Counseling

Students learn to utilize inventories and other assessment tools in order to assist clients in charting a career course for themselves. You can see how this type of counselor would be useful in a college counseling center, but they can also assist individuals who have been employed for some time but wish to make a career change. These counselors may work in private practice or in employee-assistance programs in various types of business or industry. There are only 10 universities in the United States that offer a CACREP-accredited master's program in career counseling.

Marriage, Couple, and Family Counseling

Students learn to work with families, couples, and individuals. They do so from a family systems perspective. This perspective will be discussed further in Chapter 5 but, briefly, it assumes that individuals do not operate in a vacuum but that each member of a group has an effect on another one. Using this perspective, students will learn to work with people with various emotional disorders and relationship issues. They may eventually work in social service agencies or community mental health centers or private practice or even inpatient facilities. There are 41 Marriage, Couple and Family Counseling programs in the United States. As you will see in Chapter 5 there is another whole profession titled Marriage and Family Therapy with its own history and philosophy.

Student Affairs and College Counseling

Students in this type of program are learning skills that will allow them to work in a variety of positions in higher education and student affairs. Graduates in this area typically work with college students in non-academic type of positions. For example, they may be employed in housing or residence departments assisting students with the day-to-day issues related to living at college. Additionally, they may manage student unions, provide multicultural or diversity services, coordinate orientation programs, or engage in counseling or career services. Curricula in these programs will include classes in which students can learn about the culture of higher education, how colleges and universities are organized, and how to provide leadership in policy-making affairs. There are 11 of these programs in the United States though there are an additional 22 that hold one of the soon-to-be-changed, more singular names of either College Counseling or Student Affairs.

Regardless of the specialization that you choose, typical master's programs do not have production of original research as a component to their training. While students will take courses in research methods and statistics so that they will be good consumers and evaluators of research and while there is a journal dedicated to research in the field (*Journal of Mental Health Counseling*), the production of research is not typically expected of a master's prepared therapist. However, if one chooses to go on to get a doctorate in counseling, the production of research will become more important.

So, what about a doctoral degree in mental health counseling? This is an option. Following the earning of a master's degree, you can choose to gain further education to get your doctorate (or Ph.D.)

in counseling. There are about 60 programs in the United States that offer doctoral programs in Counseling Education and Supervision. These programs are primarily for those who desire to teach at the graduate level in a university. This is the degree that many of the professors in your master's programs will hold. Professionals with this degree will be qualified to teach at a university, and/or supervise newly licensed mental health counselors. If your career goal is to simply engage in counseling and therapy with clients and not teach or supervise others, then a doctorate degree would not be necessary.

Licensing

Licensing for mental health counselors varies from state to state. You will have to check the exact requirements for the state in which you hope to work. You can do so by doing an Internet search for the State Board of Counseling in your particular state. However, there are some general rules of thumb.

Typically, following the obtaining of a master's degree, you will have to work a specified number of hours under the supervision of a licensed therapist (which often happens during graduate school with practicum and internship experiences) and then take the National Counselor Exam (NCE). This leads to initial licensure. The title given at this point also seems to vary. In some states you will be a PC (Professional Counselor); in others you will be called an LPC (Licensed Professional Counselor). After gaining further supervised experience – again this varies from state to state but is usually about 3,000 hours – doing individual and/or group counseling involving diagnosis and treatment of clients, and passing another exam, you would now be called an LPCC (Licensed Professional Clinical Counselor).

In addition to licensure, which is required to practice independently, you may apply for the National Certified Counselor (NCC). This certification is not required and is meant to illustrate to colleagues and the public that you have specialized knowledge. The only requirements for the NCC are the completion of a master's program and a passing score on the (NCE) discussed earlier. However, according to the website of the National Board for Certified Counselors (NBCC), professionals can also obtain specialty certification in the following areas: Certified

Clinical Mental Health Counselor (CCMHC), Master Addictions Counselor (MAC), and National Certified School Counselor (NCSC). There is a separate exam for each of these three areas that must be passed in order to obtain the specialty certification.

Types of Jobs for which the Degree will Qualify You

Many of the job options for mental health counselors have been described in the previous section. Indeed, the positions in which mental health counselors work will also largely depend on the type of program completed. For example, if you specialize in career counseling or student affairs and college counseling, you would likely be found working in college counseling centers or for the department of student affairs at a college or university. An addictions specialist may find employment in outpatient or inpatient alcohol and drug addiction treatment facilities. Further, those who specialize in school counseling may be employed in elementary, middle, and/or high schools.

Let me add a few general pieces of information related to jobs for mental health counselors. According to the *Occupational Outlook Handbook* in 2012 there were around 128,400 mental health counselors in the United States. About 18% of them worked in nursing and residential care facilities, about 35% were conducting outpatient treatment with individuals and families, about 12% were employed at a hospital, and about 9% held government jobs. As you can see, mental health counselors can most commonly be found in mental health centers and working as independent contractors in private practices. These type of counselors often work side by side with psychologists and clinical social workers. Remember that, once licensed, these occupations provide similar services and that the general public typically does not realize the distinction between these professions' history or training.

In summary, mental health counselors are often employed in the following areas.

- criminal justice facilities
- employee assistance programs
- crisis intervention programs

- hospitals
- community mental health centers
- private practice
- schools
- college counseling centers
- nursing homes

Earning Potential

Interestingly, the *Occupational Outlook Handbook* lists both mental health counselors and marriage and family therapists in the same entry. However, it does cite, within that entry, median salaries for each profession. The median salary reported for 2012 was $40,080 for mental health counselors. Additionally, those employed in the government sector have a median salary of $48,060, those employed in hospitals have a median salary of $43,190, those working in outpatient mental health centers earn a median salary of $40,250, and those employed in a nursing facility have a median salary of $32,530.

References

Brewer, J. (1932). *Education as guidance.* New York: Macmillan.

Dworkin, R. W. (2012). Psychotherapy and the pursuit of happiness. *The New Atlantis, 35,* 69–83.

Gladding, S. T. (2012). History of and trends in counseling. In *Counseling: A comprehensive profession* (7th ed., pp. 3–30). Boston: Pearson.

Gysbers, N. C. (2001). School guidance and counseling in the 21st century: Remembering the past into the future. *Professional School Counseling, 5*(2), 96–105.

Occupational outlook handbook (2014–15 ed.). Washington, DC: Bureau of Labor Statistics, U.S. Department of Labor.

Pistole, C. (2001). *Mental health counseling: Identity and distinctiveness.* ERIC reproduction services. EDOCG-01-09. 1–4.

Rogers, C. R. (1942). *Counseling and psychotherapy.* Boston: Houghton Mifflin.

Super, D. E. (1955). Transition: From vocational guidance to counseling psychology. *Journal of Counseling Psychology, 2,* 3–9.

5

Master's in Marriage and Family Therapy

Overall History and Philosophy of the Profession

As you read in the previous chapter, you can earn a master's degree in mental health counseling with a *specialty* in marriage and family therapy. However, you can also earn a master's degree in a marriage and family therapy program. To make matters more confusing, degrees in psychology and social work also allow you to work with marital and family clients. The real distinction has to do more with the type of training each profession receives than with the types of clients served.

According to the American Association of Marriage and Family Therapists (AAMFT), marriage and family therapists (MFTs) are mental health professionals trained in psychotherapy and family systems, and are licensed to diagnose and treat mental and emotional disorders within the context of marriage, couples, and family systems. One of the more confusing distinctions between mental health careers is that between the MFT and the mental health counselor. There are many similarities between the two. In fact, the Bureau of Labor Statistics combines them in its occupations listings.

Both professions require a master's degree and both types of graduates are qualified to diagnose and treat clients. While the course and length of their educational curriculum are similar, their theoretical orientations are somewhat different. As you have seen in the history of

Careers in Mental Health: Opportunities in Psychology, Counseling, and Social Work,
First Edition. Kim Metz.
© 2016 John Wiley & Sons, Ltd. Published 2016 by John Wiley & Sons, Ltd.

the mental health counselor, their profession developed initially from guidance counseling and, as you will see in the MFT history, much of their philosophy developed from physicians and psychologists who worked toward developing and conducting face-to-face therapy with couples and families to solve family problems and mental health issues. While MFTs will see individual clients, they work more from what is called the systems perspective and are more often engaged with families and couples. The systems perspective asserts that individuals have to be thought of in the broader context of their family (or workplace or community). The behavior of one person in the system is influenced by the behavior of others in the system. Similarly, a change in one member of system will result in changes in other members of the system. Therefore, if there are mental health issues or problems in living, the whole system needs to be considered during treatment.

An example of how this can impact treatment can be seen with clients who are struggling with a substance abuse problem. While the addicted family member is exhibiting negative behaviors, the rest of the family reacts, each in his or her own way. The parents of the family member may help the addict because they feel guilty NOT doing so. For example, parents sometimes keep enabling their addicted child because they feel that they are neglecting parental duties or responsibilities if they do not. Another family member, the little brother, may indirectly benefit from the addict's behavior because his own negative behavior is not as severe and, therefore, not noticed. For example, perhaps the brother of the addict is failing 10th grade biology but no one is really worried about this because it pales in comparison with his older brother's problem. Now, assume the addict begins the recovery process and is no longer using drugs or alcohol. Systems theorists will assert that not only did the addicted family member's illness affect the family but now so will his recovery. The previously addicted child no longer needs his parents' intervention. This frees up mom and dad to engage in other activities, namely some that involve each other. Perhaps with the newly found time they realize that they do not really enjoy each other's company. They need to start to deal with their own relationship issues. However, if their child relapses and there is renewed attention on him, the parents can go back to ignoring their own relationship problems. Further, the little brother of the addict was noticed more as his brother recovered. Parents began to attend to his falling grades and dole out consequences. If the older brother relapses, the parents may go back to minimizing the younger brother's problems. Most family systems theorists do not necessarily think that other family members would purposely sabotage successful treatment, but they will take care to note what changes the new sobriety causes others in the system to be sure that those changes don't have some unintentional effect on the recovering addict. In other words, working with an addict will always involve some consideration of the people within that addict's system.

Understand that the systems approach was not developed by MFTs though it has been embraced by them. Recall that social workers, for example, among other things, work with neighborhoods and communities in order to effect change in individuals. Additionally, psychologists were initially responsible for developing and furthering the ideas and tenets of family therapy. Many master's level social workers and mental health counselors as well as doctoral-trained psychologists use the systems approach in their work with clients. Indeed, each of these professions engages in marital and family therapy as an appropriate scope of their practice. Therefore, when early proponents of what would later be called marriage and family therapy began to try to organize themselves into a distinct profession, many of the other mental health providers objected (McGeorge, Carlson, & Wetchler, 2014).

Generally the roots of marriage and family therapy can be traced back to four major influences (Wetchler and Hecker, 2014). One of the first influences was the early social work movement in the 1920s in which solutions and remedies to poverty were sought. Many social workers at the time felt that you could best help an individual struggling with poverty by including the family in any solution. For example, Mary Richmond wrote a book entitled *Social Diagnosis* in 1917 in which she asserted that dealing with the problems of the poor necessitated working with the family as a whole. She urged other professionals to see the family early in the counseling relationship and to work to examine the "process" of the family or how they interacted. Unfortunately, this initial push was short-lived, and social workers reverted to working more with the individual until about the 1960s.

A second event that influenced the eventual creation of the discipline of marriage and family therapy was the human sexuality reform movement. This movement shone a spotlight on relationships and activities that occurred during them. In the late 1910s and early 1920s there was an initiative in both Europe and in the United States to examine and understand human sexuality in a more scientific way and to educate the general public about the findings. In 1918 Magnus Hirshfeld founded the Institute of Sexual Science in Berlin, and soon thereafter he established the World League for Sexual Reform with colleagues Havelock Ellis and August Forel. Many doctors from around the world visited the institute to learn more about human sexuality. Hirshfeld then founded the German Marriage Consultation Bureau in the 1930s. An unfortunate note about the bureau is that it was taken over when Hitler came into power and used as a venue to help decide which individuals were best-suited to procreate (Wetchler & Hecker, 2014).

Americans such as William Masters and Virginia Johnson, Alfred Kinsey, and Robert Dickenson furthered the knowledge base in the area of human sexuality in America. Kinsey wrote extensively about the sexual practices of Americans, and Masters and Johnson did pioneering work in describing the human sexual response cycle as well as common sexual disorders and their treatment. Dickenson was an obstetrician and gynecologist who participated in both research and hands-on counseling with patients. He wrote an influential book detailing the human sexual anatomy. The prevalence of this research obviously helped our understanding of human sexuality, but it also helped advance the idea that couples and their experiences were at least as important as the individual.

A third major influence on the MFT profession was the development of marriage counseling being used as a mode of therapy. The early beginning of marriage counseling, a form of therapy in which both spouses are present in the session in order to solve marital problems, was initially conducted by non-mental health providers such as the clergy, educators, or physicians. In the early 1930s three marriage counseling centers were opened by a variety of physicians: in Los Angeles, New York, and Philadelphia. The latter institution was also involved in conducting research regarding marriage and couples. While these were major accomplishments, marriage counseling still needed to develop a professional organization. The focus of the association would be to assist in developing and standardizing training programs and to organize and encourage participation in conferences that could disseminate new ideas and techniques to members. Therefore, in 1942,

Lester Dearborn, Robert Dickenson, Ernest and Gladys Groves, Robert Laidlaw, Emily Mudd, Valerie Parker, and Abraham Stone met to design and found the American Association for Marriage Counseling (AAMC). Ernest Groves was made its first president in 1945 (Wetchler & Hecker, 2014).

Despite these successful endeavors, the profession of marriage counseling saw very little progress until the 1970s. This is likely due to several factors. First, the pioneers mentioned above were strong thinkers who each had their own view of the discipline. Rubin and Settles (2012) note that these "mavericks" were difficult to "corral" into a coherent working group. A second reason for the slow progress was that there was a lack of scholarly research being conducted at that time. It is important with a new discipline that pioneers in the area research and share their findings with each other so that the knowledge base can expand and good theories can be sifted from the bad ones. It will also lend credibility to the profession. Finally, formal development of marital therapy stalled because, while there were strong proponents of it, many did not consider marriage counseling as their primary duty. For example, in 1965, 75% of the AAMC did not see marriage counseling as their primary professional duty but as an ancillary to their individual practice (Alexander, 1968). The lack of emphasis on it in their practice likely kept their enthusiasm for promoting it lower.

Then, in the 1970s, another mode of therapy, family therapy, emerged. Some of the seminal work relating to the shaping of family therapy was conducted by Gregory Bateson and his colleagues, who were studying the impact that the family environment had on the development of schizophrenia (Paratore & Nichols, 1998). The group was one of the first to make observations of the communication and organization patterns in families. While much of what was purported regarding schizophrenia and the family was later proved invalid, their research was a starting point for future pioneers in family therapy. The connection between marriage counseling and family therapy was obvious. Both believed in the relational approach and that, in order to truly help an individual, one needed to include the family. Family therapy did not focus solely on the pathology of one individual. Indeed, family therapists did not encourage having one identified patient that needed "cured" but instead recognized that each family member contributed to the functioning of every other family member.

During that time and in the decades that followed there were several influential therapists who advanced the knowledge base and practice of marriage and family therapy (Wetchler & Hecker, 2014). For example, Virginia Satir, among many other things, labeled the various roles that family members play within the family unit. Murray Bowen described the multigenerational approach, which purported that individuals learn adaptive and maladaptive behaviors as well as emotional processes from previous generations. Jay Haley was controversial as he avoided focus on insight and transference, which was the convention at the time, and he instead focused on how power and control influence the things that people do in relationships. He also felt strongly that therapists should be more directive, again bucking convention (Wetchler & Hecker, 2014).

Also in the 1970s the AAMC, marriage counseling's professional organization, changed its name to the American Association of Marriage and Family Therapy (AAMFT), incorporating both of the terms – marital and family – into its title. At this time the first journal in the area was published by the AAMFT, the *Journal of Marital and Family Counseling*, which later changed its name to the *Journal of Marital and Family Therapy*. The refining of the professional organization and the dissemination of scholarly material in a journal helped to begin to unify professionals.

Over the next couple of decades, MFTs and the AAMFT worked to help MFTs gain recognition and licensure in every state. Incidentally, much of the work was also accomplished by the California Association of Marriage and Family Therapists (CAMFT), which is an independent organization – separate from the AAMFT and its California division. It is an important entity for MFTs because many of the pioneers discussed in this chapter were from California and about half of the current MFTs reside there (Caldwell, 2010). So this organization was and is influential in furthering the causes of MFTs.

Today, marriage and family theory can be seen in many forms of psychotherapy. Remember that many mental health professionals engage in marriage and family therapy. However, if you go the route of becoming an MFT, your training will emphasize the systems approach. Your practice will then also emphasize work with families, groups, and couples. While MFTs are also qualified to treat individual clients, they will still typically address issues from a relational or systems approach.

Education

In order to become an MFT, just like for other mental health professions, you need to obtain a master's degree from an accredited program. For MFT program accreditation, you want to look for a program that the Commission on Accreditation for Marriage and Family Therapy Education (COAMFTE) has reviewed and deemed to meet accreditation standards. As described in the History section, the AAMFT is the national professional association for MFTs. Its website includes a link to all accredited programs in the country – https://www.aamft.org/ – you can click "build your career" and then "MFT programs" and search by state for accredited programs. You will notice that you can search for both master's and doctoral programs. In order to be licensed and engage in marriage and family therapy, only a master's degree is needed. However, if you have aspirations to be a clinical *supervisor* or you hope to work at the university level and/or do research, then a doctorate or Ph.D. would be needed. You might also pursue a doctorate if you want to become educated in a specific area of interest that a particular program offers. There are just over 20 accredited doctoral programs in the country and just under 90 master's programs.

A traditional master's program will generally take about 2 years to complete and include some amount of hands-on practicum hours. There will likely be coursework in research methods but typically original research production, such as a thesis, will not be required. Of course, after all that coursework and schooling, licensing is also going to be a requirement in order to conduct therapy.

Licensing

According to the AAMFT website, all states now license MFTs. As with mental health counselors, some states have really only developed licensing criteria in the last few years. To illustrate, the AAMFT website notes that in 1986 there were 11 states that regulated MFTs and, by 2009, all 50 states regulated the profession in some way. Currently, there are 48,000 MFTs practicing in the United States and Canada. As with the other mental health professions, the rules regarding licensing vary somewhat from state to state. This website, http://www.mft-license.com/#licenserequirements, enables you to click on your state to view its specific requirements. In some states, MFTs have their own licensing board. In other states, MTFs have been incorporated into pre-existing social worker and/or counselor licensing boards.

In general, in order to be licensed as an MRT you would need to earn a master's degree and then engage in a set number of supervised clinical practice hours. Following this, you would apply for and achieve a passing score on the Association of Marital and Family Therapy Regulatory Boards (AMFTRB) Examination in Marital and Family Therapy. The exam is a 4-hour, 200-question, multiple choice exam that is designed to ensure the test taker has mastered a sufficient amount of material related to the practice of marriage and family therapy.

Types of Jobs for which the Degree will Qualify You

MFTs can be found working in many of the same types of agencies as a clinical social worker or a mental health counselor. The AAMFT surveyed its members in 2011 to try to determine, among other things, where an MFT was most likely to be employed (see http://www.aamft.org/imis15/documents/careers_in_mft_2012.pdf). Results indicated that:

- 49% (the vast majority) worked in private practice
- 15% worked in an agency – this is most likely some type of community mental health center
- 11% worked in an academic setting, likely teaching or supervising, and/or conducting research
- 4% worked in hospitals
- 4% worked in religious-based outpatient centers
- the remaining percentages were employed in schools, and residential treatment facilities, or the respondent answered "other."

These numbers must be understood with caution as they represent the places of employment in which AAMFT members reported working. Note that membership in the AAMFT is voluntary, so a survey of its members will tap a select group of people. It is possible that the numbers would change somewhat if every MFT, not just those who belonged to AAMFT, were surveyed.

Remember that the *Occupational Outlook Handbook* groups mental health counselor and marriage and family therapist in the same category. It does, however, give a breakdown within the entry for jobs held by MFTs. According to the 2012 *Occupational Outlook Handbook*:

- 25% of MFTs are engaged in work in individual and family services
- 24% of MFTs work in outpatient clinics
- 22% of MFTs work in a governmental agency
- 13% of MFTs work in hospitals or nursing facilities

Overall, the majority of MFTs seem to be most likely working in some type of outpatient facility, such as a private practice or a community mental health.

Earning Potential

The AAMFT survey discussed above also asked respondents about their income. As you will see, the types of questions asked to get their survey results vary from the way the *Occupational Outlook Handbook* asks about and reports income. Both sets of numbers will be listed here. First, AAMFT members reported the following:

- 9% earned less than $25,000
- 22% earned between $25,000 and $50,000
- 28% earned between $50,000 and $75,000
- 23% earned between $75,000 and $100,000
- 18% earned over $100,000

These numbers seem high, and it is likely that the AAMFT is tapping into later-career MFTs who earn more money than early career MFTS who have not yet done things like pay to be a part of professional association. Also, remember that about half of the MFTs also reported working in a private practice. It is possible that some of them own their practice and make income off therapists who work within their practice. Finally, remember that a great number of MFTs reside in California, where the cost of living is likely higher. This could potentially skew the numbers.

The *Occupational Outlook Handbook* reports the numbers a bit differently. These are the numbers reported in most other sections of this text, and they are probably the ones to best compare apples to apples. The *Handbook* reports the median salary for the top five industries in which these professionals work. The numbers are as follows:

- $67,230 – Government jobs
- $45,090 – Offices of health practitioners
- $44,130 – Outpatient care centers
- $41,960 – Individual and family services
- $37,450 – Nursing and residential care facilities

In summary, those working in some type of outpatient facility or private practice, which are the most likely places of employment for MFTs, are typically earning on average a salary in the low to mid-$40,000s.

References

Alexander, F. (1968). An empirical study on the differential influence of self-concept on the professional behavior of marriage counselors. Unpublished doctoral dissertation, University of Southern California.

Caldwell, B. (2010). AAMFT, AFTA, CAMFT, IFTA, and more: A primer on MFT associations. Retrieved from http://www.psychotherapynotes.com/uncategorized/aamft-afta-camft-ifta-and-more-a-primer-on-mft-associations/.

McGeorge, C. R., Carlson, T. S., & Wetchler, J. L. (2014). The history of marriage and family therapy. In J. L.Wetchler & L. L.Hecker (Eds.), *An introduction to marriage and family therapy* (2nd ed.). New York: Routledge.

Occupational outlook handbook (2014–15 ed.). Washington, DC: Bureau of Labor Statistics, U.S. Department of Labor.

Paratore, J. B., & Nichols, M. (1998). *Family therapy, historical overview.* Boston: Allyn & Bacon.

Richmond, M. E. (1917). *Social diagnosis.* New York: Russell Sage Foundation.

Rubin, R. H., & Settles B. H. (2012). *The Groves conference on marriage and family: History and impact on family science.* Ann Arbor, MI: University of Michigan Press.

Wetchler, J. L., & Hecker, L.L. (2014). *An introduction to marriage and family therapy* (2nd ed.). New York: Routledge.

6

Substance Abuse/Chemical Dependency Counselor

Overall History and Philosophy of the Profession

This chapter is a bit deceiving because you doesn't usually get a degree in substance abuse or chemical dependency. Typically, a person becomes certified or, in some cases, licensed in it. There are two important caveats here. First, all licensed mental health professionals can work with clients suffering from substance abuse. I will expand on this further in the Education section. Second, recall that master's degrees in counseling programs have areas in which you can specialize. Addiction counseling is one of those areas in which a mental health counseling master's student can specialize, and it was mentioned briefly in Chapter 4. The reason that I am including a whole chapter on this subfield is that there are also other ways to work in the addictions field. A master's degree is required in order to earn some types of certification. Other types of certification require less education. These variations will be discussed in the Education section.

For now, let me expand on the history of this area. Before we do that, however, please note that this area of treatment is referred to in several ways, that is, substance abuse counseling, chemical dependency counseling, or addiction counseling. The term utilized is not reflective of any hierarchical order but simply reflective of the fact that each state and sometimes each agency has its own way of referring to clinicians

Careers in Mental Health: Opportunities in Psychology, Counseling, and Social Work, First Edition. Kim Metz.
© 2016 John Wiley & Sons, Ltd. Published 2016 by John Wiley & Sons, Ltd.

who specialize in working with individuals with alcohol and other drug dependencies. I will use the terms interchangeably in this chapter.

Addiction counseling has its origins in what is referred to as "lay therapy." That is, those who treated clients with substance abuse issues were not necessarily trained in the field. These "recovering" individuals did not have training in substance abuse and typically did not have training in any mental health profession. More specifically, the treatment providers were often simply individuals who had suffered from and overcame their own addiction. This approach is sometimes termed the "wounded healer" approach. In the 1910s Courtenay Baylor appears to be one of the first treated and recovered clients to be hired into the treatment center where he had been a patient. This situation occurred in large part because mainstream medicine and mental health organizations did not yet view substance abuse as a medical problem but as a moral failing (Hagedorn, Culbreth, & Cashwell, 2012) and such groups largely neglected these afflicted individuals. Therefore, alcoholics began to rely on others who had overcome alcoholism for nonjudgmental, supportive treatment.

The wounded healer approach became even more prominent following the formation of Alcoholics Anonymous (AA) (Hagedorn et al., 2012). Alcoholics Anonymous was created in 1935 by Bill Wilson (always referred to as Bill W. since last names are not used in AA). Bill W. was a stockbroker whose struggles with alcoholism led him to have great difficulties in his job. After many false starts, he was led by a friend to a religious group, the Oxford Group, who believed that alcoholism could only be "cured" by God. The Oxford Group was organized and run by Frank Buchman and adhered to several critical tenets or principles, including asking participants to agree that their situation was hopeless and out of control and that they must practice honesty and make amends for past mistakes. Interestingly, the AA website's history section notes that Bob W.'s introduction to the Oxford Group came to him from a friend, Ebby T., who joined the Oxford Group at the urging of his friend, Roland H., a wealthy man who had sought help from none other than Carl Jung. Jung determined that Roland's case was "medically hopeless" and referred him to the Oxford Group hoping that a spiritual cure may be what he needed.

With support from religious and spiritual sources, Bill W. achieved recovery and maintained sobriety. He then met and helped a doctor,

Dr. Bob, who was also struggling with alcoholism. Bill helped Bob recover from his alcoholism using a similar spiritual philosophy and support to his own. The two men took their theory and philosophy to Akron City Hospital in Ohio, where they helped other men recover from alcoholism. Bill W. and Bob S. became the originators of what would become Alcoholics Anonymous. Note that from the beginning the "wounded healer" model was fundamental to treatment.

Later, in the 1950s, the AA philosophy evolved into what was termed the Minnesota Model of treatment (Borkman, Kaskutas, & Owen, 2007). The Hazelden treatment center, founded by an AA member in Minnesota, was one of the first formalized treatment centers to use the tenets of this model. The Minnesota Model leaned heavily on the 12 Steps of AA, which Bill W. had originally formulated by expanding on the basic principles of the Oxford Group. The model adheres to the disease model of alcoholism, which holds that alcoholism is a disease and that it is chronic and progressive. The goal of treatment in this model is nothing less than total abstinence from alcohol. Lay people with no formal training continued to be the treatment professionals who worked with those afflicted with substance abuse problems (Hagedorn et al., 2012).

Hagedorn et al. (2012) further explain that, once the American Medical Association (AMA) adopted its formal disease model concept of alcoholism in 1956, other professionals began to take more notice of it and of treatments for it. For example, in the 1970s, the National Institute for Alcoholism and Alcohol Abuse (NIAAA) and the National Institute for Drug Abuse (NIDA) began developing formal training programs (though not ones that required any advanced degree) in substance abuse in order to educate professionals about addictions and the treatment of those who suffered from them. Additionally, the inclusion of addiction in the AMA disease nomenclature meant that third-party payers (insurance companies) would pay for the treatment of it. This made treatment of alcoholism more attractive to potential treatment professionals as well.

As you can guess, the landscape of addiction-helping professionals began to change to a large degree. There were still paraprofessionals who had no formal training in substance abuse but had struggled and recovered from their own addictions; however, there were now individuals who had completed training programs in chemical dependency and substance abuse but who did not necessarily have personal experience with abusing alcohol or other drugs. And finally, there was a third group of helping professionals who were a blending of the first two groups. They were recovering from addiction and had engaged in formal education and training to treat it in others. There was much debate about and subsequently much research to help determine which of these treatment professionals were best-suited to work with the addicted (Culbreth, 2000).

Today, most agree that treatment professionals need to have some formal treatment in substance abuse in order to work effectively with clients. Moreover, this is true for the treatment of any client, not just ones suffering from an addiction. Treatment professionals must understand and stay abreast of any new developments in the areas in which they practice. So, an understanding of and training in advances in the area of addictions is needed to be an effective treatment provider. Hagedorn et al. (2012) list four advances in addictions that have occurred over the last several decades. They argue that, due to these advances, specific training and credentialing is imperative.

First, he notes that a treatment goal of abstinence is no longer the only goal in addictions treatment. The theory of harm reduction (versus abstinence) has as its goal a modification of drinking behavior rather than just the cessation of it. This is a somewhat controversial theory but one in which more research is being conducted and more techniques are being designed. Therefore, treatment professionals need training to understand whether the theory is valid and, if so, how to determine which individuals would benefit from harm reduction and which would not. Second, there has been a significant amount of research examining people's ability and willingness to make a change in their behavior. Treatment success may have a great deal to do with understanding where a person is in their change process (Prochaska, DiClemente, & Norcross, 1992). A knowledge of this change process is important in the treatment of many different types of clients but especially substance abusing ones, since very little treatment can occur until the client agrees to make a change. Third, researchers and practitioners have realized that a person's addiction is often influenced by other mental health problems (e.g., depression) and it is important to take this "dual diagnosis" into account during treatment. This means that an effective treatment professional would need to have a working knowledge of other mental health disorders as well as an understanding of substance abuse. Finally, and most recently, there has been a movement to consider the idea that other behaviors besides alcohol and drug abuse may also be viewed as and treated as addictions. These so-called process addictions or behavioral addictions include problem gambling, sex addiction, shopping addiction, and Internet addiction. Research is being conducted on these potential disorders now. In fact, recently, gambling was included as a disorder in the *Diagnostic and Statistical Manual-V* (DSM-V.) Given all of these advances and developments in the area of substance abuse, it is now essential that a treatment professional has more than a history of his or her own recovery in order to be a successful therapist.

It was accepted that proper training of addictions treatment professionals was important, though how to train such professionals was initially unclear. As with other professions discussed in this text, the field became more organized professionally when a national association was organized. In 1974 the National Association of Alcoholism Counselors and Trainers (NAACT) was founded, and it began to recommend some initial training standards. Its goal was to unify substance abuse counselors into a professional organization with common objectives and standards for training and practice. In 1982, the organization became the National Association for Alcoholism and Drug Abuse Counselors (NAADAC) and aimed to unite professionals working for positive outcomes for substance abusers. Then, in 2001, the organization changed its name to "NAADAC, the Association for Addiction Professionals" in an effort to include the various types of addiction professionals that existed. It is a global organization that represents the interests of over 85,000 addiction specialists. Its members focus on prevention, intervention, and treatment of chemical dependency. However, none of these entities spell out specific, accepted training standards for professionals in the field.

Education

There are a variety of ways to be educated in the treatment of addicted clients. First, as mentioned earlier, every licensed mental health professional is qualified to work with substance abusing clients. However, there are some (Hagedorn et al., 2012) who are critical of these programs for not creating some type of credential or specialty designation that students could earn by taking extra coursework or practicum hours in addiction. As has been mentioned before, these mental health professions do not get an extra credential for learning more about depression or schizophrenia, so many believe that an extra specialty designation for addictions would not be necessary either.

One mental health profession HAS come up with a way to have its students specialize in addiction. Do you remember the various specialties that a master's level mental health counselor can earn? CACREP is the body that accredits master's level counseling programs and it now has one titled Addictions Counselor. Therefore, a second way to work with this population is to earn ar mental health counselor master's degree specializing in substance abuse treatment. There are not many training programs with this designation yet, so it may be difficult to find such a program.

A third way to work with chemically dependent clients is to earn some type of credentialing by taking advanced classes in the area but not necessarily earning a bachelor's degree. This is a step above the "wounded healer" and below someone with graduate training. You may be able to find schools that offer associate degrees in this type of coursework.

Licensing

As mentioned above, for several decades there has been an encouragement toward being credentialed in some fashion in order to work with chemically dependent individuals. Originally, the credentialing process meant that individuals with any professional or nonprofessional background completed workshop hours in courses related to addiction. While this was a step above simply having been recovered oneself as a prerequisite for working in the substance abuse area, it was still imperfect. Most notably, this requirement meant that individuals participated in classroom-type training but they were not tested on the knowledge learned there. This meant that it was difficult to tell who was learning what. This led to a push to make formal training a necessity. Indeed, there are now requirements in each state detailing how to get either credentialed or licensed (depending on the state and level of experience) as a substance abuse counselor. I must note here that, of all the professions explained thus far, this was one in which it was the most difficult to find succinct information. You really have to search your state substance abuse or chemical dependency board.

Remember though that there are three ways to make addiction therapy part of your scope of practice. In the first way, as a licensed mental health professional there would be no need for further credentialing, though getting a special credential may make you stand out from other job applicants. In the second way, specializing in addiction counseling as a mental health counselor, you would also already be licensed to practice if you follow the mental health counselor licensing requirements. For the third way, having less than a graduate degree, there is now in most states a way to get credentialed. Overall, it is typically possible to get a lower-level credential for education short of a graduate or even an undergraduate degree. Higher levels of credentialing are available for those who have earned a bachelor's degree and even higher levels for those with a master's degree. You will need to check the professional board in the state in which you wish to reside.

To give an example of what type of requirements are out there for licensing/credentialing, I am including the requirements for the state of Ohio, according to the Ohio Chemical Dependency Professional Board. Note the various levels of training represented. A credential can be earned in the following ways in Ohio:

CDCA: *Chemical Dependency Counselor Assistant*

Phase I Forty hours of chemical dependency-specific education in the following areas:

- Addiction Knowledge (5 hours)
- Treatment Knowledge (9 hours)
- Professionalism (6 hours)
- Evaluation (3 hours)
- Service Coordination (4 hours)
- Documentation (3 hours)
- Individual Counseling (5 hours)
- Group Counseling (5 hours)

Phase II   Hold a Phase I of CDCA for at least 10 months.

Thirty hours of chemical dependency specific education (completed after obtaining CDCA Phase I status) in the following areas:

- Addiction Knowledge (5 hours)
- Treatment Knowledge (3 hours)
- Professionalism (3 hours)
- Evaluation (3 hours)
- Service Coordination (3 hours)
- Documentation (3 hours)
- Individual Counseling (5 hours)
- Group Counseling (5 hours)

LCDC II: Licensed Chemical Dependency Counselor II

- An associate's degree in a behavioral science or nursing OR a bachelor's degree in any field.
- 1 year (2,000 hours) of chemical dependency counseling-related compensated work or supervised internship experience.
- 180 hours of chemical dependency education in 9 specific content areas.
- 220 practical experience hours in the 12 core functions. This may be completed as part of your work experience requirements.
- Successful completion of the Alcohol and Drug Counselor (ADC) examination or completion of the Examination Waiver Form.

LCDC III: Licensed Chemical Dependency Counselor III

- A minimum of a bachelor's degree in a behavioral science or nursing.
- 1 year (2,000 hours) of chemical dependency counseling-related compensated work or supervised internship experience.
- 180 hours of chemical dependency education in 9 specific content areas.
- 220 practical experience hours in the 12 core functions. This may be completed as part of your work experience requirements.
- Successful completion of the ADC examination or completion of the Examination Waiver Form.

LICDC: Licensed Independent Chemical Dependency Counselor

- A minimum of a master's degree in a behavioral science with documentation of coursework in 10 specific content areas.
- 1 year (2,000 hours) of chemical dependency counseling-related compensated work or supervised internship experience.
- 180 hours of chemical dependency education in 9 specific content areas.
- 220 practical experience hours in the 12 core functions. This may be completed as part of your work experience requirements.
- Successful completion of the ADC examination or completion of the Examination Waiver Form.

LICDC-CS: Licensed Independent Chemical Dependency Counselor-Clinical Supervisor

- A minimum of a master's degree in a behavioral science with documentation of coursework in 10 specific content areas.
- 2 years (4,000 hours) of chemical dependency counseling-related compensated work or supervised internship experience.
- 1 additional year (2,000 hours) of work experience as a clinical supervisor of chemical dependency counseling services.
- 180 hours of chemical dependency education in 9 specific content areas.
- 220 practical experience hours in the 12 core functions. This may be completed as part of your work experience requirements.
- 30 hours of clinical supervisory education.
- Successful completion of the ADC and Clinical Supervisor (CS) examinations or completion of the Examination Waiver Form.

As you can see, at least in Ohio, one can hold a license with or without an undergraduate or graduate degree. I encourage you to search the licensing board in your state to determine its requirements. Ohio's website also includes a list of places that offer some of the initial non-undergraduate treatment hours one needs to get the most basic credential.

Remember that if you have already earned a degree and licensure in one of the areas that we have already discussed (clinical or counseling psychology, social work, or counseling) you are already qualified to treat clients with substance abuse. A credential is not a necessity if you hold a license in one of those mental health areas. So why get the credential? Two reasons. First, it tells the public and your coworkers that this is an area in which you have chosen to become better versed. Many clinicians find that they gravitate toward working with certain populations of clients. Most will earn continuing education credits in those areas (workshop or coursework hours earned in areas of their choice in order to maintain their license). This enables them to get the most current information regarding a particular disorder and its treatment. In the case of substance abuse, there is an actual credential that can prove you have done so. A second reason to earn the credential is that some agencies may require that you have that extra specialized training in order to consider you for employment. If it isn't a requirement, it may make you more marketable when compared with other applicants.

Types of Jobs for which the Degree will Qualify You

The type of job for which you will be qualified will obviously depend on the level of training/credentialing you have received. However, below please find a list of typical facilities in which substance abuse professionals might be employed.

Outpatient treatment centers   Professionals with advanced degrees may work in outpatient mental health centers, such as community mental health centers or private practices. They can practice individual or group therapy with people suffering from addictions. If such professionals do not possess a graduate degree and a license, it is unlikely that they would be able to conduct individual or group therapy.

Residential or Inpatient Treatment Centers

Substance abuse professionals may be employed in a residential facility. In such a facility, clients live at the treatment center for a prescribed period of time, where they receive individual and group counseling. While master's level counselors would obviously be needed in this setting, there are also likely opportunities for those with lower levels of training. Clients need attention and interventions throughout the day and throughout their stay.

Criminal Justice Facilities

It should come as no surprise that many inmates struggle with chemical dependency. There may be job opportunities to work with them during their incarceration to help treat their substance abuse.

Probation and Parole Agencies

A probation officer who has knowledge and understanding of the causes and effects of addictions would be more able to assist those in his/her supervision.

Earning Potential

As you no doubt already realize, the salary of substance abuse professionals will depend on not only the type of agency in which they work and the area of the country in which they live, but it will also depend on the level of training they have. Professionals who do not have a graduate degree will make less than those who do. On average, according to the *Occupational Outlook Handbook*, in 2012 the median salary for substance abuse professionals was $38,520. The lowest-paid employees earned $25,140 while the highest-paid employees earned $60,160.

References

Borkman, T., Kaskutas, L., & Owen, P. (2007). Contrasting and converging philosophies of three models of alcohol/other drugs treatment. *Alcoholism Treatment Quarterly*, 25(3), 21–38.

Culbreth, J. R. (2000). Substance abuse counselors with and without a personal history of chemical dependency, *Alcoholism Treatment Quarterly*, 18(2), 67–82.

Hagedorn, W. B, Culbreth, J. R., & Cashwell, C. S. (2012). Addiction counseling accreditation: CACREP's role in solidifying the counseling profession. *The Professional Counselor,* 2(2), 124–133.

Occupational outlook handbook (2014–15 ed.). Washington, DC: Bureau of Labor Statistics, U.S. Department of Labor.

Prochaska, J., DiClemente, C., & Norcross, J. (1992). In search of how people change: Applications to addictive behaviors. *American Psychologist,* 47(9), 1102–1114.

7

School Psychologist

Overall History and Philosophy of the Profession

School psychology has its roots in the social reforms that occurred in the late 19th and early 20th centuries. As discussed in prior chapters, the Industrial Revolution changed the landscape of social and economic issues in America. The reforms that occurred included compulsory education, juvenile courts, child labor laws, and the development of both mental health and vocational guidance. At this time, children attending school came from very diverse backgrounds with very diverse needs. A few schools began to conduct physical and mental testing on their students and, by 1910, there were special education departments in many schools. The person who helped determine which students qualified for these programs was soon to be termed the school psychologist.

These early conceptions of school psychologists were largely formulated by Lightner Witmer. In previous chapters, the importance of this early pioneer in psychology has been discussed. His influence also stretched into and makes him a pioneer in the area of school psychology. First, a little more background on Witmer is warranted. Witmer had as a mentor Wilhelm Wundt. Recall that Wundt developed/designed the first psychology laboratory. He was trained in philosophy and physiology and he took the experimental method utilized in scientific study

Careers in Mental Health: Opportunities in Psychology, Counseling, and Social Work, First Edition. Kim Metz.
© 2016 John Wiley & Sons, Ltd. Published 2016 by John Wiley & Sons, Ltd.

and applied it to psychology or the study of humans and the human mind. D'Amato, Zafiris, McConnell, and Dean (2011) point out that Witmer, after being trained by the research-oriented (versus practice-oriented) Wundt, still, somewhat surprisingly, had more applied interests than purely basic research ones. Specifically, he was interested in studying learning problems in children. This is an area one might not have expected Witmer to pursue given his rigorous training in empirical methods. However, he used his considerable knowledge in the scientific method to learn more about the population whom he hoped to help versus only focusing on the application of the sparse existing knowledge about these types of children. D'Amato et al. (2011) state that "with Witmer's leadership, psychology moved off the couch and into the laboratory. This was the opposite direction Dr. Sigmund Freud seemed to be advocating in his book with Breuer (1895) entitled *Studies on Hysteria*." Recall that Freud, while advancing the applied practice of psychology, relied very little if at all on scientific methods to draw his conclusions and formulate his theory.

Witmer noted that, before he could develop any interventions for the children, he needed to understand the basis of their difficulties. Therefore, he examined them more empirically in order to be able to design interventions (D'Amato et al., 2011). Witmer presented his ideas about testing and understanding children's learning to the APA at its annual meeting in 1896. In his presentation he outlined his ideas for this new specialty in psychology. Overall, he advocated that both normal and learning-impaired children be studied using both empirical and clinical methods. He also indicated a need for psychological clinics to assist children with learning problems. He then encouraged students in both education and medicine to engage in observation of normal and mentally retarded children. Finally, he advocated for a new profession in psychology that would work with schools and the medical community treating children with learning-related issues.

Another pioneer in this area was G. Stanley Hall. His focus on children and learning was even more research-based. One of his contributions was to gather normative data about learning for various types of children. That is, he believed that, before we can determine if an individual child has a learning problem, we must know at what level the typical child of the same age and group is capable of achieving.

The combination of Hall and Witmer's work created the foundation for the testing movement and school psychology.

The development of the first intelligence test is often credited to British psychologist Sir Frances Galton. He measured children's sensory and motor skills in an effort to determine their level of intelligence. Subsequently, French psychologist Alfred Binet was asked by the French government for assistance in making determinations about which children would have the most difficulty with formal education. He worked with colleague Théodore Simon to develop an instrument that would do that. They found that tests of practical knowledge, memory, reasoning, vocabulary, and problem solving seemed to be better predictors of academic success than the sensory and motor abilities measured by Galton in his intelligence tests. Their work was brought to America by H. H. Goddard, who was the director at the Vineland Training School for Feeble-Minded Girls and Boys (note, how appropriate language and labels for people have evolved over time). Goddard was traveling in Europe when he was introduced to the scale. Unfortunately, Goddard's intentions for the use of the test were not all admirable. He hoped to use it to determine "feeble-mindedness" and to encourage those found to qualify as such to not "breed." In 1916 Lewis Terman, also an American psychologist, desired to use the test with adults, not just children. He worked at Stanford University at the time, so he named his adult adaptation of the test the Stanford–Binet. This remains the name of the test today.

As has been discussed previously, World War I also had a significant impact on psychology and testing in general. The military needed to screen incoming soldiers quickly in order to determine to which type of job specialty they would be most suited. Lewis Terman, Robert Yerkes, and other psychologist collaborators developed the Army Alpha and Army Beta tests. Both tests were designed as group administered measures. The Army Alpha test measured verbal ability, numerical ability, ability to follow directions, and basic knowledge of information. The Army Beta test was designed for soldiers who were non-English speaking or were unable to read. About 1.5 million recruits were administered the Army Alpha and Beta tests for selection, placement, and training purposes. The tests were prototypes for future military cognitive screening measures. Specifically, they were the precursors to the cognitive test utilized by the Armed Services, the

Armed Services Vocational Aptitude Battery (ASVAB). According to the official ASVAB website, there were tests used subsequent to the Army Alpha and Beta tests in different branches of the military. However, in 1974, the Department of Defense mandated that all branches of the service would use the ASVAB to screen new recruits for suitability and to place them in military occupations that best matched their aptitude and ability. The widespread and consistent use of these psychological measures by the military helped solidify the relevance of tests of individual ability and achievement. Additionally, they helped to solidify and define the primary role and function of school psychologists who were responsible for designing, validating, implementing, and interpreting them.

In the midst of the development of these Armed Services' aptitude tests, other milestones were being reached by school psychologists. In 1925, New York University established the first school psychology training program. While the APA existed at this time, school psychologists were excluded from membership because their training was primarily undergraduate in nature and the APA insisted upon a doctoral degree for membership. Recall from an earlier chapter, however, that after World War II there was a surge in APA membership. During this increase, the APA expanded its division structure and in 1945 Division 16 – School Psychology was created. Obviously, this recognition gave the field more credibility.

The next major development in intelligence testing, which would ultimately affect the duties of the school psychologist, occurred when David Wechsler created his own intelligence measurement instrument in 1955. Wechsler agreed with Binet that a variety of abilities make up a person's intelligence and so each ability needs to be measured. However, he was dissatisfied with several aspects of the Stanford–Binet assessment measure. For example, the Stanford–Binet resulted in a single score that Wechsler thought limited the understanding of a person's true intelligence. In addition, the Stanford–Binet was not designed to be used with adults. Finally, he felt that the Stanford–Binet relied too much on timed tasks. Therefore, Wechsler developed his own instruments. His work includes a test for children (WISC – Wechsler Intelligence Scale for Children), for preschoolers (WPPSI – Wechsler Preschool and Primary Scale of Intelligence), and for adults (WAIS – Wechsler Adult Intelligence Scale). All of the tests contain multiple subtests and result in scores in different areas of intelligence as well as producing an overall, full-scale IQ score. The subtest scores are particularly useful for school psychologists in that they are integral in identifying learning disabilities.

Recall from Chapter 1 that a turning point in psychology history was the Boulder Conference held for 2 weeks in 1949 in Boulder, Colorado. The aim of the conference was to establish standards for training graduate students and evaluating graduate programs in clinical, counseling, and school psychology. Baker and Benjamin (2000) points out that, after World War II and the number of psychological-related problems that existed, many more practitioners were needed. In addition, there was an influx of trainees in the newly returned soldiers who were able to attend school by virtue of the newly offered GI bill. Traditionally, university Ph.D. training programs (in any discipline) were focused more on scientific research and experimentation; however, many psychologists, especially those in subspecialties such as school psychology and clinical psychology, felt they had a duty to be more applied in nature in order to best serve their clients. As you know, the result of the Boulder Conference was the development of the scientist-practitioner model of training. Training programs would stress both the applied or practice side of psychology, but they would also stress the research or science side of the discipline.

This new training model could potentially impact school psychology training programs as well as the clinical and counseling training programs. However, there were not many school psychologists at that time, and Hynd (1983) notes that clinical psychologists were more hesitant to apply their training and knowledge in school settings. Therefore, Division 16, School Psychology, organized a conference to examine training issues specific to school psychology as well as to clarify the role and goals of the evolving profession in general. The conference, termed the Thayer Conference for the hotel in which it was held, took place in 1954.

One of the first issues addressed at the conference was the lack of school psychologists. Survey data gathered by Cutts (1955) indicated there was only one school psychologist for every 1,000–3,000 students. A second issue addressed was the lack of training sites for school psychologists. At the time there were only 5 university doctoral training programs and 13 sites that trained students at lower levels than the doctoral rank (Hynd, 1983). Finally, participants at the Thayer Conference examined and made recommendations about the training standards of school psychology programs. Each program was teaching on/training in the areas it saw as important, but there was no national unity or standardization across the programs. This resulted not only in uneven training but also in confusion about where each graduate could be employed because titles and certifications across programs were also varied. Advocates knew that poorly trained or inappropriately placed graduates could be a detriment to elementary and high school students whom they were trying to help, and that this could harm the profession's reputation.

Recommendations that resulted from the Thayer conference included, first, an agreed-upon definition for school psychology, as related by Cutts (1955): "psychologists with training and experience in education who use their specialized knowledge of assessment, learning and interpersonal relationships to assist school personnel to assist the experience and growth of all children and to recognize and deal with exceptional children."

Second, in addition to defining school psychology, the committee strived to describe the most important functions of a school psychologist. One such function was to engage in assessments of children and use the results to design remediation plans. Another function was that school psychologists should engage in appropriate research to further the knowledge base of the profession. Note, however, that many contended (and still do today) that there was not sufficient time for school psychologists to conduct relevant research. Further, it was recommended that school psychologists would work to serve the greatest number of students possible. To that end they should help advise school teachers and school personnel in the design and evaluation of curriculum and teaching methods. This also would entail initiating and maintaining good working relationships with teachers, principals, and other school personnel (Hynd, 1983).

Finally, the committee tried to reach a consensus about the training of school psychologists. Several ideas took hold. First, the conference participants decided that, while doctoral-trained school psychologists were needed, so were master's level professionals. Therefore, two levels of training were advocated. However, the distinction between the doctoral and sub-doctoral specialties quickly became blurred, and the inclusion of the non-doctoral professionals alienated the specialty as a whole as well as upsetting members of the APA (D'Amato et al., 1989). This led to the creation of their own professional association, the National Association of School Psychologists, in 1969. The establishment of this association enabled school psychologists around the country to unite with common goals. A second training issue the Thayer group weighed in on concerned encouraging states to put standards in place for training and certification. Third, they encouraged graduate student engagement in practicum and other hands-on experiences as a requirement for training programs. There was also some debate about whether an appropriately trained school psychologist should have teaching experience. In the end that recommendation was not made, as it was felt that a good background in education would suffice.

In 1975 Public Law 94-142, the Education for All Handicapped Children Act, was passed. At this time, many children with disabilities were underserved in U.S. schools. This Public Law assured that the rights of disabled children and their parents were protected. This law also made the activities of the school psychologist more necessary and prominent in schools.

In 1980, the Spring Hill conference was convened and participants focused again on role, identity and training issues. They also examined changing societal influences, such as public pressure to make schools more accountable, racial discrimination, economic disparity in schools and communities, and how those issues impacted the school psychologist. Recommendations were made to strengthen identity and training standards. It was thought that increasing the number of state organizations and their contact with the national organization (NASP) would be beneficial to the profession. Indeed, the number of state school psychology associations increased from 17 in 1970 to 48 by 1989.

The role of school psychologists today is typically to work in schools consulting with teachers, parents, and administrators to provide counseling, assessment, and outreach to pupils. Their role is significant (as is the role of teacher) because children spend such a large percentage of their day at school as compared to home. Adults who have authority and influence over them are very important in the student's development. Additionally, while student learning is the obvious goal of school systems, it does not happen in a vacuum. Students are coping with family, social, and peer issues, which can all have an impact on school performance.

School Psychologist versus School Counselor

You should be aware that there is another profession, the school counselor, who obviously has a similar title, works in the schools, and may share some responsibilities with the school psychologist. Therefore, confusion often exists between the two professions. I'd like to try to delineate the differences between the professions here. These differences mostly concern their responsibilities at the school and the training that they receive. Keep in mind, however, that in practice there is some overlap in duty. For example, both may be involved in one-on-one counseling with students. Additionally, roles for each profession may vary from school district to school district and from school to school.

In terms of the purported duties of each profession, the biggest differences concern the population with which each work. School psychologists typically work with students who have special education needs such as learning disabilities, while a school counselor typically works more with the general population of students. Therefore, the school psychologist will work more with students who have potential for qualifying as special needs students. He or she may conduct psychological assessments to ascertain whether the student does or does not meet criteria for qualifying for special education services. Once qualified, the school psychologist will have a significant role in monitoring the progress of these students, as well as assisting in the planning of academic and or behavioral/emotional interventions and in composing reports regarding the student's functioning. At times these positions may not be funded with general school district funds but by monies directed specifically to special education services.

As noted above, school counselors typically are engaged with the entire general population of students. They help students cope with day-to-day challenges and encourage good decision-making in the social and academic arenas, such as career or college choice decisions.

For example, in middle schools and high schools, a school counselor may work with students to resist peer pressure or to become educated about drugs and alcohol, or may devise programs designed to curb bullying. In an elementary school, he or she might conduct social skill groups. In 2003, in an effort to clarify the role and identity of school counselors, the American School Counselor Association constructed a National Model for School Counseling Programs. Among other things it outlined the duties and roles that a school counselor should perform. Those duties include activities such as designing student academic programs, counseling students with excessive tardiness, absenteeism or disciplinary problems, collaborating with teachers regarding potential guidance curriculum lessons or regarding suggestions for classroom management, and managing student records according to state and federal standards.

The training of a school psychologist and a school counselor is different. I will describe more fully the education of school psychologists in the next section. And I have discussed the education of a school counselor as a specialty in Chapter 4. Recall that school counseling is one of the areas in which a graduate level master's counseling student can specialize. In general, school psychologists need more schooling – at least 60 graduate credit hours and very often a Ph.D. as well as supervised internship hours – than a school counselor who needs 48 credit hours plus a lesser number of internship hours.

Education

Obviously, to become a school psychologist, one must first obtain a bachelor's degree. Typically, students will major in either psychology or education during their undergraduate years. A fewer number may major in sociology or child development or social work. If you major in an unrelated field, it would be helpful to minor in one of the majors listed above.

The next step is to obtain a graduate degree; the progression of graduate work is a little different for the school psychologist than for the clinical or counseling psychologist. However, similar to clinical and counseling psychology, licensing is imperative. Therefore, while I am giving you the basics for what it takes to become a school psychologist, you will want to double check the requirements for your specific state to be sure you are meeting those requirements.

The first decision to be made regarding graduate education is whether you want to obtain an M.S., an Ed.S., or a Ph.D. I will discuss the Ed.S. in a moment, as it is a type of degree that has not been an option for the other mental health professions discussed thus far. The NASP website includes a link that delineates various types of training available for school psychologists (http://www.nasponline.org/students/degreefactsheet.pdf) but they are also described here.

Master's Degree

One option is to obtain a master's degree. Typically, master's programs have requirements for classwork and internship/fieldwork that can take up to 3 years to complete. The total number of credit hours needed is typically *under 60 semester hours*. The drawback of this degree is that it does not make one eligible for licensure following graduation. Obviously, this will make finding appropriate employment more difficult. For this reason, there are fewer of these programs in existence unless they lead directly to obtaining a more advanced degree.

Specialist Degree

Another option is to obtain a specialist degree. This can be done in two ways. First, by completing a master's program that requires *at least 60 semester hours* and *a minimum of 1,200 internship hours* (versus the *less than 60-hour* option discussed above). Second, by earning an Educational Specialist (Ed.S.) degree, which also requires *at least 60 semester hours* and *1,200 internship hours*. Various programs may offer one or the other degree option.

The Ed.S. degree is basically a step above a master's degree (of less than 60 hours) and a step below a doctoral degree. Therefore, graduates are awarded the degree after they have completed a master's in education, which takes about 1 year, and then complete more coursework as well as an internship. This typically takes an additional 2 years. If this is the program for you, it is recommended that you choose a program that has been approved by the NASP. This professional organization approves school psychology programs to ensure that they meet agreed-upon standards for training and provide opportunities for extensive and properly supervised internship experience. The school in which the program is housed (e.g., the School of Education) should also have been accredited by the National Council for Accreditation of Teacher Education (NCATE).

The advantage to obtaining a specialist degree is that graduates will be eligible for national certification in school psychology, as a specialist degree is considered the entry-level degree for school psychologists. Another advantage is that this degree option takes less time than a Ph.D. (discussed next), and students are able to get involved in internship opportunities very early in their schooling. A final point that may be considered another advantage is that, as you will see in the "Licensing" section, individuals who earn at least 60 hours and complete an internship by obtaining a master's or specialist degree are eligible for licensure. No state in the country licenses master's level psychology in any area except school psychology. Therefore, no master's level psychology degree holder can use the title "psychologist" or engage in "psychological work." The sole exception to this is the master's of at least 60 hours and the specialist degree, both of whom can be called "school psychologist."

A Doctoral Degree

Another option is to obtain a doctoral degree in school psychology. This can be accomplished by earning either a Ph.D., a Psy.D., or an Ed.D. Like doctoral degrees in other areas of psychology, it requires approximately 5–7 years of coursework. A Ph.D. program also requires the completion of original research projects (a thesis and dissertation) as well as a 1-year internship. A Psy.D. has similar coursework and internship requirements with less emphasis on conducting original research. At this level, Ph.D. and Psy.D. graduate programs should have accreditation by the APA and would ideally have approval by the NASP. There are about 60 APA-approved Ph.D. school psychology programs in the United States and only 5 APA-approved Psy.D. programs. There are an even smaller number of programs that allow a student to get a dual degree in clinical (or counseling) psychology and school psychology. The Ed.D. programs are housed in departments of education and focus more on skills and theory related to educational practice versus a focus more on clinical application of the theory.

There are two major benefits to obtaining this more advanced degree. How important these benefits are to you will depend on your career goals. First, a Ph.D. or Ed.D. means that you are qualified and eligible to teach at university level. Psy.D.s will still have a more difficult time gaining employment at a university because of the differing emphasis on research that their programs have, which has been discussed in prior chapters. A second benefit is that earning a Ph.D. or Psy.D. in school psychology makes graduates eligible to sit for the Examination for Professional Practice of Psychology (EPPP). Passing this test as well as other state licensing board requirements would enable an individual to work in a school and/or engage in clinical practice. These are two big benefits to an advanced degree but, if you do not desire to teach or engage in clinical practice, they are unnecessary for you and a specialist degree is all that is really needed. If you are unsure of your final career goals, there are some graduate schools that have specialist programs and doctoral programs. If you desire, you can begin with a specialist degree and then move on to the doctoral program. If this appeals, be sure to look for schools that offer both programs. A full listing of school psychology programs can be found on the NASP website.

Licensing

As is true with the other professions that have been discussed, each state sets its own requirements for licensing, so you have to research your own state's rules. Be aware that in school psychology, you should be seeking *credentialing* (rather than licensing) as a school psychologist. Most states will require that an individual hold a specialist degree (either an M.S. of at least 60 hours or an Ed.D.) or a Ph.D. and have completed an internship. Fulfillment of these criteria will typically make students eligible to sit for an exam, which in most states is the PRAXIS School Psychologist Test. Achieving a passing score on this test will also be a requirement for credentialing. Additionally, some states may require a certain number of postgraduate supervised work prior to licensure. Upon completion of all of these requirements, a person is registered as a Nationally Certified School Psychologist (NCSP).

For those students who took the doctoral route there is another option, discussed above, of being licensed to conduct clinical work by taking the EPPP, the same exam that clinical and counseling psychologists must take. Check your state's specific rules for this. As discussed earlier, if your intention is to strictly work in schools, then it would not be necessary to take the EPPP. However, if you desire to have the option of seeing clients in therapy outside of the school setting, then passing the EPPP would be necessary.

Types of Jobs for which the Degree will Qualify You

School Psychologist

Individuals can be employed in public and private schools. The exact nature of their job is often dictated by the needs and finances of the school district. For example, some districts may employ one school psychologist who will rotate through several schools in the district throughout the week. Other districts may have one school psychologist at each of their elementary, middle, and high schools. Many times their salaries are pulled from the special education budget, which means that their job responsibilities will center on individual students with special learning and behavioral needs. Serving such students may require both assessment and counseling as well as work on interdisciplinary teams to help craft and follow through with plans to assist students in need.

Administrative or Supervisor Positions

School psychologists can also be employed in administrative or supervisory roles. This often occurs after gaining experience as a practicing school psychologist. Responsibilities could include program development/evaluation, direct supervision of school psychologists, administrative duties such as hiring, firing, budgeting, staff evaluation, and policy development.

University Faculty

While school psychologists are typically employed in elementary, middle, and high schools, they may also work in a university setting as a faculty member if they went the route of earning a Ph.D. The primary responsibility of a faculty member would be to train new school psychologists and to engage in research in the areas related to child and adolescent issues.

Earning Potential

Earning potential is a bit more difficult to estimate for school psychologists. First, the *Occupational Outlook Handbook* published by the Bureau of Labor Statistics does not make a distinction between clinical and counseling psychologists and school psychologists, instead incorporating them all into the same category. To cloud matters further, remember that those who work in schools are often paid based on the budget of the school district. Furthermore, many school psychologists may work on a 10- or 11-month contract versus one that lasts an entire year. Notwithstanding those variables, the median salary given for clinical/counseling/school psychologists in 2012 in the *Handbook* was $67,650.

Additional insight about income can be gained from the NASP, which conducted a survey about the salary of its members in 2009 (Castillo, Curtis, & Gelley, 2012). They reported the mean salary of responding school psychologists in various roles. Those on 200-day contracts who worked in schools as practitioners (doing assessment, counseling, outreach, etc.) earned a mean amount of $71,320. School psychologists who were employed as university faculty, who were likely also on a less-than-year-long contract, reported a mean salary of $77,801. Finally, NASP members who worked in administrative positions earned a mean salary of $93,258. Note that those working in administration are more likely to work on year-long contracts. These data are a bit dated and are only representative of school psychologists who are also members of NASP; however, they still give a snapshot of salary possibilities.

References

Baker, D., & Benjamin, L. (2000). The affirmation of the scientist-practitioner: A look back at Boulder. *American Psychologist, 55*(2), 241–247.

Castillo, J. M., Curtis, M. J., & Gelley, C. (2012). School psychology 2010: Demographics, employment, and the context for professional practices – Part 1. *Communique, 40*(8), 28–30.

Cutts, N. E. (1955). *School psychologists at mid-century.* Washington, DC: American Psychological Association.

D'Amato, R. C., Zafiris, C., McConnell, E., & Dean, R. S. (2011). The history of school psychology: Understanding the past to not repeat it. In M. A. Bray, & T. J. Kehle (Eds.), *The Oxford handbook of school psychology* (pp. 9–62). New York: Oxford University Press.

Hynd, G. W. (1983). *The school psychologist: An introduction.* Syracuse, NY: Syracuse University Press.

Occupational outlook handbook (2014–15 ed.). Washington, DC: Bureau of Labor Statistics, U.S. Department of Labor.

Unit 2
Strategies and Skills

Now that you have examined the details of a variety of mental health professions, I would like to share with you career information that is useful despite which of those professions you may choose. In fact, some of the information may help you in your decision to even pursue a career in one of these fields at all. I will begin with a chapter that is designed to help you examine your motivations to working in this field. It will hopefully help you see which of these motivations are fitting and useful and which of them might be inappropriate or misguided. Next, I can scarcely have a conversation with a student or a class without stressing the importance of critical thinking. Therefore, I will include a chapter discussing the importance of using this skill for your career and for your life in general. Then, I will touch on the ethics of doing counseling or therapy with clients. This is an area in which you will receive MUCH more information on during your schooling but I believe that having a quick primer on the types of things that are expected of you ethically as a mental health professional will help you discern whether these types of careers are for you. Next, I include a chapter regarding things to do to increase your chances of getting into a graduate program. Admission to many types of programs can be competitive so I want to give you suggestions for how to stand out among other applicants. Finally, I am including a chapter that discusses some specifics about life after attaining a degree and licensure. In that

Careers in Mental Health: Opportunities in Psychology, Counseling, and Social Work, First Edition. Kim Metz.
© 2016 John Wiley & Sons, Ltd. Published 2016 by John Wiley & Sons, Ltd.

chapter I will touch on continuing education and malpractice insurance as well as a movement to have therapists engage in therapy via the internet or other technology. Additionally, I will give you some details regarding psychologists possibly gaining prescription privileges. Remember that only a psychiatrist can prescribe medicine but there is a movement to allow psychologists the opportunity to do so as well. If this becomes commonplace, this could have an impact on mental health professions in general.

8

Why (and Why Not) to Pursue a Mental Health Professional Career

There are good and not so good reasons to strive for a career in one of the mental health professions. In this chapter I delineate what some of the good and bad motivations are in order to help you decide if this field is really for you. The information here will also illustrate the characteristics of a good therapist.

Why TO Pursue a Mental Health Career

1. You are genuine and have a caring personality. Possessing these characteristics appears to be one of the things that contributes to success in therapy. Researchers discovered this when they were trying to determine which type of therapy might produce the best results. That is, what therapy works best? Psychodynamic therapy where the client talks about their childhood and tries to unearth unconscious motivations? Behavioral treatment that gets the client to focus on things that might be rewarding or tries to get the client to identify which elements help maintain their negative behavior? Cognitive treatment that encourages clients to attend to the way that they perceive events occurring in their life so that they see things more positively than negatively? Or humanistic treatment that focuses on allowing the client to explore and determine their own course of action by being attentive and in

Careers in Mental Health: Opportunities in Psychology, Counseling, and Social Work,
First Edition. Kim Metz.
© 2016 John Wiley & Sons, Ltd. Published 2016 by John Wiley & Sons, Ltd.

tune with them? These are really the main theoretical orientations for conducting therapy, and many have sought to determine which is more effective or worthwhile. Studies of the literature in this area of examining the effectiveness of various treatments have shown that most find an insignificant difference between therapeutic modalities (Wampold, 2015). That is, that all the treatments seem to produce similar outcomes. Further, what research has also shown is that certain therapist characteristics, irrespective of what treatment paradigm the therapist utilized, seemed to have a more positive effect on client success (Wampold, 2015).

These therapist factors are often referred to as "non-specific" factors, in contract to the specific factors present in a particular therapy. The personality of the therapist seems to be one of those "non-specific" factors (Reisner, 2005). Those therapists who were better at building rapport or forming a therapeutic alliance seem to be more likely to have successful clients. For example, Ahn and Wampold (2001) reviewed the literature and conducted a meta-analysis of 27 studies that involved therapeutic intervention meeting their set criteria. They found no effect size between the studies, meaning that no treatment modality or therapeutic technique seemed to work better than another. Yet clients showed improvement. This improvement is thought to be related to the non-specific factors that enhance the therapeutic alliance between the client and the therapist. Characteristics of the therapist that seem to be related to an ability to form a therapeutic alliance include flexibility, honesty, respectfulness, trustworthiness, confidence, alertness, friendliness, warmth, and openness (Ackerman & Hilsenroth, 2003).

Incidentally, researchers have also looked at the different types of therapists (psychologist, social worker, etc.) to see if one had more positive outcomes than another. One of the more well-known studies in this area was actually conducted by *Consumer Reports* ("Mental health: Does therapy help?" 1995), a popular magazine that publishes unbiased reviews of services and products used by many Americans. Seligman (1995) discussed several significant finding from that study. First, results indicated that individuals who received some form of therapy fared better than those who received nothing. Second, longer-term therapy clients fared better than shorter-term therapy clients. Third, their finding echoed previous research that indicated that no treatment modality worked better than another. Fourth, patients who had to limit the amount of therapy received due to constraints placed by insurance or managed care fared worse than those patients who did not have those constraints. Finally, based on patient overall improvement scores (a number that could range from 0 to 300), patients who were seen by psychologists (220) versus psychiatrists (226) versus clinical social workers (225) seemed to fare about the same. That is, these differences between improvement scores were not significant. Clients of what the researchers termed marriage counselors (208) did not seem to fare as well in this particular study. Despite lesser scores for the marriage counselor in this one study, it should be noted that most mental health professionals did indeed produce similar satisfaction ratings from their clients.

In conclusion, it seems to matter less which type of therapist you are and which type of therapy you choose to practice. Instead the "non-specific" variables of warmth and ability to form a therapeutic alliance seem to be important to client success and satisfaction with treatment. Keep in mind that this does not mean that the information you learn in whichever graduate program you choose is not important and essential. You must know the nuts and bolts of human behavior. It does say, however, that those with warm and caring personalities who apply these nuts and bolts will be more successful.

2. *You have good coping skills.*   It is a taxing (though rewarding) job to talk to people in depth and at length about their problems, especially if the client population with which you work is particularly difficult (e.g., sexually abused children, substance abusers, domestic violence victims, domestic violence perpetrators, etc.). However, even if your clients have more benign presenting problems (adjustment disorders, relationship break-ups, oppositional children, job stressors, etc.), the emotional toll on a therapist can still be high. Remember, that you will typically be talking to people who are experiencing very negative events in their life. Clients don't set up appointments to discuss the raise they received at work, or to let you know that their teenager just got accepted to their first-choice college, or to inform you that they are in a very happy marriage right now. And when they start to feel better and their life seems more on track, therapy is usually terminated. Put bluntly, you typically see people at their worst.

A steady diet of other people's sadness or weaknesses has the potential of bringing even a well-adjusted person (therapist) down. Therefore, mental health professionals must be sure to take care of their own mental health and to not take on the emotions of their clients. If you have flown on commercial airlines, you will have heard the flight attendants give their safety talk at the beginning of the flight. When they discuss the oxygen mask that may be released if cabin pressure is compromised, they tell people to put their own mask on first and then assist others with their mask. They say this because, obviously, you can't assist people in that type of emergency if you can't breathe yourself. The exact same rule applies to therapists. You need to be in reasonably good mental health before you can effectively help others with their issues. That does NOT mean that you will not have sadness, strife, problems, or trauma in your own life. It means that you will utilize the coping skills that you will likely be teaching your clients to help yourself through the difficulties so that you are now able to help others with theirs.

I regularly teach a human development class at my university, and when I get to the adult development chapter and we discuss stressors in adulthood, I often have my undergraduates take a few minutes to shout out their favorite coping skill to combat stress in their life. A few popular ones are: listening to music, going for a drive, reading, sleeping, eating, shopping, journaling, exercising. A few rebels will shout out: drink alcohol, have sex, punch something. By the way, these "rebel responses" can actually be good coping skills IF they are used in moderation (a glass of wine instead of two bottles) or IF they are modified slightly (punch a pillow instead of a person). My class usually can, in just 5 minutes or so, get about 40 or 50 coping skills written on the board. Then I tell them that typically we rely on only two or three of these skills to help us when we are upset or angry or depressed or are otherwise in need of a way to manage or cope. I challenge them – as I am now challenging you – to attempt to use others in your daily life. The more coping skills you have the better! This is because you can't use those two or three favorites in every situation. For example, when you get a bad grade on a test you can't use your favorite coping mechanism of, say, sleeping, because you have two more classes to get to and then volleyball practice. You need a skill that you can use right then – in the moment. Taking a few deep breaths, exercising by walking fast to your next class, squeezing a stress ball in your pocket, or making a call to vent to your mom might do the trick.

You also have to be sure that the skill really works for you. For example, some people like to listen to certain kinds of music when they feel stressed. However, sometimes "that" kind of music might actually raise our heart rate and blood pressure and make us angry and stressed all over again. The same is true of journaling and venting to a friend. For some people those tactics help them get the issue "off their chest" and they feel calmer and more adjusted afterwards. For other people, those activities only serve to remind them of just how bad they feel or how angry they are, and they wind up feeling worse than before they listened to the song, wrote in the journal, or vented to mom. In order to have good coping skills, you have to figure out what works best for you. You are likely going to be helping your clients determine this same thing for themselves. But remember that you have to put your mask on first!

3. You are a good listener and show empathy to others.   Listening skills are probably a therapist's best tool. You have to be able to hear things that people say as well as things they don't say. It is important to practice active listening, being able to reflect an individual's comments/thoughts/feelings back to them, to ensure that you are understanding them completely and to let the client know that you truly heard them. Incidentally, this is a useful skill to utilize in every-day relationships as well.

Additionally, a good therapist should be empathic. Having empathy is not the same thing as feeling sorry for someone. Having empathy is being able to understand and identify with someone's experiences. This doesn't necessarily mean that you agree with their behaviors or their decisions, just that you can understand how they have come to them. For example, someone with an addictive disorder is making choices (to drink too much, to steal, to lie) that you do not agree with. However, you can empathize with how difficult it is to stop these behaviors now that the addiction has developed. Or, think of an eating-disordered client who thinks she is fat when she is sorely underweight. If you empathize with her, it doesn't mean that you simply feel sorry for her or that you agree that she is overweight. It means that you have an appreciation for how debilitating it would be to hold such irrational thoughts in her head on a day-to-day basis, or for how difficult it would be to alter her behavior if her mind continues to tell her such misinformation.

Many times clients simply need to feel understood. Do you remember when you experienced what you now see as a trivial problem? Perhaps when you broke up with a boyfriend or girlfriend in middle school? It may have frustrated you when your parents told you that "there are lots of fish in the sea" or "you are young, you will have many more relationships." You may have gotten the sense that they didn't understand the gravity of what you were feeling. Your friends, on the other hand, probably did "get it." They understood your pain and commiserated with you. *They had empathy.* Now, remember, your parents were correct – there are lots of fish in the sea and you will meet someone new. However, you wanted to be heard and understood and not have your feelings minimized. This is what clients need to hear from you first and foremost. After they realize that you understand them, they will be much more receptive to your insights or suggestions or interpretations of the situation.

4. You have good communication and interpersonal skills.   If you want to work in this field, you should have a strong ability and strong desire to talk to and interact with people. Interactions with clients are sometimes kind and empathic, sometimes conflictual or confrontive, sometimes emotional and intense, sometimes exciting and lively, some-times thoughtful and quiet (or even silent). If you are comfortable interacting in all of those situations, you will be a more effective thera-pist. In addition, you must be able to do this with a variety of types of individuals. That is, with those individuals who share your ideals and values and the ones who may not. For example, I have heard clinicians say that they cannot do therapy with sex offenders. That behavior is just too contrary to their own value system. Now, I'm not saying that every social worker, mental health counselor, substance abuse counselor, psychologist, or school counselor must work with sex offenders. However, some must! How will we protect our children if we don't find a way to communicate with and treat someone who engages in this type of behavior? Working with difficult clients such as sex offenders, domestic violence perpetrators, or abusive parents is part of the job, and your communication and interpersonal skills will be necessary if we are to help those clients find alternative and more socially acceptable ways to behave. If your communication and interpersonal skills are strong, you will be able to interact with and effect change in many different types of clients.

Note that under the heading of "good communication" we should include good written communication. This does not mean that you have to be a great creative writer or that you will be writing lots of 10–12 page research papers. It does mean that you should be able to effectively and succinctly share your thoughts about and progress with a client. You may be asked to write reports for schools, for the courts, for other treatment personnel, or for insurance companies.

Why NOT to Pursue a Mental Health Career

1. You want to be rich.   You have seen the salary estimates for all of the professions discussed so far. The numbers are respectable and with those salaries one can live comfortably; however, these salaries will not allow you to live extravagantly. Certainly the longer you are employed and the more experience you have, the more you will earn. As noted in Unit 1, there is a wide variety of places to be employed and some places boast better salaries and benefits than others. Begin by looking at job boards and websites to get a feel for the types of jobs and salaries that are available in the location in which you hope to live.

Many young students who want to prepare for a career to "help people" also have a dream of having their own practice as they understand that they can earn over $100 per hour. As noted earlier, therapy sessions are billed at a rate approximating just over $100 per hour; however, it was also noted that if it is not your practice you will only receive a percentage of this amount (between 50% and 60%) depending on your credentials. If your dream is to own the practice, then the percentage of money that you retain as owner must be utilized for things such as: rent; utilities; staff to greet clients, schedule appointments, bill, and disperse insurance payments; an answering service or some alternative to handle after-hours calls; marketing and/or advertising, web design; and a host of other incidentals. Some of these tasks therapists can do themselves, but then the time they spend doing those tasks cannot be spent seeing clients and earning money. This is not to say that owning a practice cannot become lucrative at some point. With enough independent contractors working for you, there will be a point where you will be able to make a tidy sum. If owning your own practice one day is a goal of yours, think about taking a few business classes while you are earning your undergraduate degree.

Some of you may decide that you do not want to own a practice but just work for one, and you are busy multiplying the cut you think you might be able to earn by a 40-hour work week. HOWEVER, please keep in mind that it is almost impossible (unless you have no other interests in life) to see 40 hours of clients each week. This schedule implies doing therapy 8 hours a day, 5 days a week. This is difficult to do from an emotional and energy standpoint and, honestly, your last and next-to-last client will likely suffer due to your mental drain by the end of the day. Second, the chance that every client who is scheduled will keep their appointment is slim. Therefore, you would almost have to schedule 10 hours' worth of clients in order to ensure that 8 of them keep the appointment. You may charge clients for missed appointments or if they have not given enough notice in which to schedule someone else in their time slot, however, you may NOT charge insurance companies (it would be considered insurance fraud to charge for an appointment that did not take place). That means that a cancellation fee would be a full charge for a client versus the much smaller co-pay that most would normally pay. Just like you have missed appointments for valid reasons, so will your clients, and it will be difficult to consistently collect every missed-appointment fee.

The other thing to consider if you work as an independent contractor is that you do not receive the typical benefits that you will likely get if you work directly for an employer or agency. First, you would probably not get a paid vacation benefit. The positive about this is that you can adjust your schedule to take as much vacation as you like (or as much as would ethically allow you to tend to the needs of your clients). However, you will not be earning money while you are away. Second, as an independent contractor, you are responsible for paying the portion of employment tax that an employer would typically pay. This is money that is given to you in a paycheck but that you will have to pay back to Uncle Sam at the end of a quarter or a year. So your check will appear very large as no tax dollars are withheld. It is tempting to spend that large check. However, if this is how you are paid one day, be sure that you are disciplined enough to save enough of your check to make the tax payment. Otherwise, you will end up owing thousands of dollars to the federal and state government when tax day arrives. Third, independent contractors, since they are not technically employees, are typically not offered health insurance. You are responsible for purchasing on your own insurance, which is much more expensive than any premium you would pay to a traditional employer to be a part of their health insurance plan. Finally, your cut of the pay for seeing a client is not typically given to you until your practice collects the money from the client or the insurance company. This may take a longer or shorter time depending on the insurance company and on how efficient your billing staff is. It does mean, though, that your paychecks will not be consistent and that you could earn a good sum one month and a much smaller amount the next. It also means that it may take a month or two to be compensated for work done today. This is again where discipline (and good budgeting skills) come in. That is, if you get one large check this month, you may need to save some of it for next month instead of spending it all because next month's check may be much lower.

This section is not meant to discourage you from helping clients by working as an independent contractor. It really isn't. This is one of the jobs that I do and, while the above obstacles exist, they can be overcome. For example, as long as you become very proficient and disciplined at budgeting, you can easily learn to spend and save your monthly income appropriately. Further, the freedom and flexibility of working for yourself is a very positive aspect of this job. It also lends itself well to part-time work, so those who only want to work a few hours a week can do so as an independent contractor and still make a respectable amount of money, while most agency-type work will require a full-time commitment. The health insurance problem can be remedied by opting in to the new federal universal health care. Alternatively, if you are married, your spouse may be able to cover you under his or her health insurance plan.

2. You want to work from 9 to 5.   Many job opportunities in agencies, especially government jobs, may actually be 9 to 5 jobs, so you would be safe here. However, if you plan to work doing some type of outpatient work with clients, this will not totally be the case. While you can typically set your own schedule in private practice or sometimes at a community mental health center, you need to remember that your clients likely have jobs or school. It is difficult, for example, to have a working mom keep an 11 a.m. appointment every Wednesday. While she might be able to do that for a one-time dentist appointment, recurring ones with a therapist will be more difficult, and she will likely want an evening or weekend time. If you hope to see children, adolescents, or families it is even more important that you have availability outside of the school day. Therefore, most of the psychologists, social workers, and mental health counselors who do individual or group therapy in a private practice or mental health center will work at least one or two evenings each week and/or work weekends.

3. You want to socialize and talk to other people at your job.   This comment may seem like it's in the wrong section. After all, isn't your job going to be to talk to people all day? Well, sort of. ... Clients are going to talk to you and you need to respond to their concerns and issues, but the exchange will rarely (or should rarely) be focused on anything that relates to you personally. That means you get to talk all day but not about yourself! Now, this is especially true if you work in a private practice or a community health center type of agency. While you will have co-workers in such agencies, they will really only be people that you see in passing at the "top of the hour" when you are in a central office area writing case notes and trading the file of your last client for the file of your next one. It is difficult to hold meaningful conversations during these few minutes. You and your co-workers are like "ships passing in the night."

This was made most clear to me after my father, who resided with me during a battle with colon cancer, died. I was working at a mental health center at the time and, when he passed away, the office staff called to cancel and reschedule about 15 clients with apologies noting that my father had died. When I returned to work and eventually saw those 15 clients, not one of them inquired about my father or offered condolences. Briefly, probably because it was a very sad time for me anyway, I was upset that they hadn't offered sympathies of some kind. However, I recovered quickly. Those clients aren't supposed to offer me condolences. Their sessions are about them and their issues. My issues should not interfere with their progress or their time in session. The story is meant to exhibit the rather isolating nature of this job that seems so social. It's also meant to encourage you to be sure that you have adequate support in your personal life. One reason I recovered quickly from my annoyance with my clients is because I had a stable support system outside of work and didn't really need the "strokes" from people at work. So be sure that you nurture the relationships with friends, significant others, and/or children. Doing so will make you a better mental health professional.

4. You need to see the results of your work immediately.   If you are an immediate-gratification type of person (if you would "eat the marshmallow" – Google "Mischel's Marshmallow Test" if you don't understand the reference), this may not be the right job for you. While there will be times when you are able to see immediate results in your client's life, sometimes you don't really know what impact you are having. If you engage in therapy, clients will often stop coming for appointments, and you won't be sure if that is because they feel they have been helped or because they feel they have *not* been helped or if it just got too difficult to make time for appointments with all their other obligations. Some places of employment, by their nature, don't allow you to follow up with the client. For example, if you work in a correctional facility, unless the client gets re-arrested, you may not know for certain how emotionally healthy they are back in their everyday life. Further, if a medical social worker at a hospital places a patient into, for example, a rehab center after a bad fall, the social worker will now likely be out of the loop and another social worker at the rehab center will determine what happens next with the client. So you will not necessarily be aware of his or her progress.

Rest assured, you WILL experience more immediate gratification some of the time. After all, this is why most of you are hoping to work in one of the mental health professions. You WILL help people. There will be times in which you do see progress in a client or when they express relief that they are feeling better since beginning therapy. Or you will find out that a student whom you helped work through struggles at middle school is graduating from high school at the top of his or her class. Those things WILL happen. However, sometimes you will have to be satisfied with the idea that you have hopefully "planted a seed" and that, even without continued contact, the seed will grow.

5. You are good at telling people what to do. One of the misconceptions of therapy held by early therapists in training and the general public is that mental health providers give advice and recommend a particular solution to a problem. On the contrary, the therapist's job is not to "tell people what to do" but to help clients make a determination of the best course of action for themselves. Let me use divorce as an example. I have had many marital couples in therapy and invariably they ask the question, "Doc, should we just get divorced?" By the way, they often ask this after the first or second session. As if my Ph.D. and I can discern the answer after 2 hours of knowing the couple in a more effective manner than they can, after knowing each other for decades. Divorce is not my (or your) call to make – though you may have an opinion on it! However, the choice to get divorced entails many other consequences besides a date at the courthouse. For example, consider a woman who has been married for 30 years and discovers her spouse has been unfaithful. As a young therapist with strong values related to adultery, you might be tempted to ADVISE her to leave her spouse. However, doing so involves the undoing of 30 years of life together, including children, grandchildren, a home, investments, etc. It is up to the wife to decide if having an unfaithful husband is grounds to undo all of that. And it very well may be for her! But it also may not be. That is what therapy can help her discover: What are the things that she is willing to sacrifice in order to keep other things on track and progressing? Or is that sacrifice too big? Additionally, infidelity may be the presenting problem, but it is likely that there are other precipitating factors that led to it in the first place. Perhaps remediating them will end the unfaithfulness and allow the couple to move forward with each other.

6. You are anxious to begin learning about and solving your own or your loved ones' emotional problems. Many students desire to go into a mental health profession because they have experienced a serious trauma or mental illness. Sometimes they have been helped greatly by a therapist and that has motivated them to want to help others in return. That motivation is a noble one. However, you must be sure that you really are trying to "give back" and not attempting to solve your own (or a loved one's) problems. This can actually get in the way of successful treatment of clients. You have to be sure you can help clients come to good conclusions about their own issues without letting your personal feelings influence their decisions. This is not to say that you have to be 100% mentally and emotionally stable to be a mental health professional. If that were the case, we would have a serious staff shortage! However, it is important to understand and work through your own psychological issues so that you can have clear judgment when working with others.

References

Ackerman, S. J., & Hilsenroth, M. J. (2003). A review of therapist characteristics and techniques positively impacting the therapeutic alliance. *Clinical Psychology Review*, 23(1), 1–33.

Ahn, H., & Wampold, B. E. (2001). Where, oh where, are the specific ingredients? A meta-analysis of component studies in counseling and psychotherapy. *Journal of Counseling Psychology*, 48(3), 251–257.

Mental health: Does therapy help? (1995, November). *Consumer Reports*, pp. 734–739.

Reisner, A. D. (2005). The common factors, empirically validated treatments, and recovery models or therapeutic change. *The Psychological Record*, 55, 377–399.

Seligman, M. (1995). The effectiveness of psychotherapy: The *Consumer Reports* study. *American Psychologist*, 50(12), 965–974.

Wampold, B. (2015). *The great psychotherapy debate: The evidence for what makes psychotherapy work*. New York: Routledge.

9

Critical Thinking

I mentioned early in my Introduction that I very rarely pass up a moment to discuss and hone critical-thinking skills in my students. This moment is no different. And believe it or not, it very much applies to the topic of the text. My whole reason for writing this book was to help you critically think about the career you are choosing. You should not just pick a path because Aunt Susie is a social worker or because your favorite professor said you should be a psychologist or because the graduate school option closest to your home is a marriage and family therapy program. You should instead gather information (which can include Aunt Susie, your professor, and MapQuest, but not be limited to them) and then evaluate that information without judgment by analyzing evidence and questioning arguments and conclusions.

Critical thinking is sometimes an art that gets discouraged as you get older. A good example of critical thinking is asking "Why?" Remember as a kid that you asked why the sky was blue, why mommy's tummy was so big, and why you had to eat your vegetables? Those were all good questions. You were trying to understand the world around you and not just accept what others told you: "everyone needs fruits and vegetables" or "because I said so." As you might guess, this critical thinking in children can become overwhelming for the adults in their life. Therefore, parents and teachers often unintentionally discourage it

Careers in Mental Health: Opportunities in Psychology, Counseling, and Social Work,
First Edition. Kim Metz.
© 2016 John Wiley & Sons, Ltd. Published 2016 by John Wiley & Sons, Ltd.

and instead encourage a more blind following of instructions and doing what you are told. In some ways this is necessary and advantageous when we are trying to teach a large number of concepts to large groups of kids. Their conformity and lack of questioning may make for a more efficient transfer of basic knowledge; however, it can make for a poor critical thinking, poor judgment, and poor decision-making.

So I challenge you to try to work on increasing your critical thinking so that you can make more informed choices about your career and about a million other things that you will encounter in your lifetime. What follows are some basic principles that you should adhere to when trying to ensure clear, critical thinking. I will try to illustrate these principles with examples from daily life as well as with more professional/career-related examples. Many of these principles are discussed in introductory psychology textbooks such as Wade and Tavris (2014).

Distinguish between Real Science and Psychobabble

Go to the "self help" section in your local bookstore or search "self help" on Amazon, and you will find no shortage of authors giving advice about how to improve your marriage, raise your children, lose weight, or increase your brain power. Some of these books are based on real research while others are just someone's opinion on how to accomplish such tasks. Your choice of purchase should be one that describes and summarizes relevant clinical research in the area, notes the limitations or weaknesses of the ideas, and then draws relevant conclusions. Too often something that sounds good and seems plausible has no science behind it. Sometimes the science is conducted after the fact, and the original theory is debunked. However, that is often too late. People are often very resistant to altering their original theory.

We can see how this happened centuries ago when many, especially within the Catholic Church, believed that the Earth was an immovable mass that the sun revolved around. Given a human's perspective on and experience with the world, the theory sounded good and plausible. It also seemed to match up to information gleaned from the Scriptures. Then came pesky Galileo with his telescope and his science and his tenacity. He proved that the Earth was not the center of the universe but actually revolved around the sun and was vocal about his findings. However, this "proof" did not matter to most people. They stuck to their original belief, the thing that they had always been told – the Earth was the center of the universe. In fact, in 1633 Galileo was convicted of heresy by the Church.

There is a modern-day example of this resistance to give up a strongly held notion. I am guessing that you have heard of the autism/vaccine controversy. The controversy concerns whether childhood vaccinations are causing autism in children. The original potential connection was written about in an article for the *Lancet* by Andrew Wakefield and colleagues in 1998. Despite the small sample size (12 children) and questionable research design, the study received a great deal of publicity and some parents began to perceive a connection between their child's autism and the MMR vaccine they received. For the next 10 years researchers tried to replicate Wakefield's results but were unable to do so. However, many parents had already begun to refuse the MMR vaccine for their children. It was also discovered that there were ethical issues with the study, namely that Wakefield's work was funded by lawyers whose clients were suing MMR vaccine manufacturers. This was a serious conflict of interest that also made Wakefield's results more dubious. The *Lancet* eventually retracted Wakefield's article in 2010 and Wakefield was found guilty of ethical, medical, and scientific misconduct (Flaherty, 2011), but the damage had been done. Researchers continued to look for scientific evidence that might prove vaccines cause autism – no scientific causal factors have been found (Madsen et al., 2002; Marwick, 2001; Taylor, Swerdfeger, & Eslick, 2014). While you would think that the public would no longer believe in the connection between autism and vaccines, many parents continued (and continue) to refuse to vaccinate their children for mumps, measles, and rubella for fear of the child developing autism. These diseases, which had been all but eradicated, are now resurfacing and causing illness and even death in some children. Additionally, because the way vaccines work is not to render every recipient 100% protected but to create a "herd immunity" (Google this if you are unclear of the very important meaning of "herd immunity"), even children who have received vaccines are also now susceptible to illness. Many, such as Flaherty (2001), feel as if the gravity of the communication of misinformation cannot be overstated.

He asserts, "The alleged autism-vaccine connection is, perhaps, the most damaging medical hoax of the last 100 years."

The point of the rather lengthy explanation of the vaccine/autism controversy is to illustrate one major way that unscientific and unproven information – psychobabble – can be detrimental to people. It shows that we have to think critically about information not just accept it and/or retain it because it has taken root in our consciousness. I could fill another text with other examples of ways that people accept without question theories and ideas. If you want to read about them, research "facilitated communication" or "rebirthing" and see the kind of damage a lack of critical thinking can inflict. In the meantime, just keep this issue in mind as you read the psychological and mental health literature for your studies and career: Try to distinguish between psychobabble and true science. You can do that by following some of the guidelines listed next.

Always Ask Questions

I mentioned earlier that we often train kids to not ask questions, but that this damages critical thinking. You can't uncover the truth without asking questions. Take politics, for example. Can you trust everything a politician running for office says? If he purports that he supports increasing funding to the schools, it would be advantageous to research his record of voting on education issues to see where he really stands versus take his word for it. Further, if you watch an infomercial late one sleepless night and you hear that new pills will help you lose weight without cutting back on your food or adding exercise, should you automatically grab your credit card and buy? Obviously, the answer is "no." You should do more research and ask more questions about the product and its use. Try to find studies that randomly assigned individuals to an experimental and control group, that is, a group of people who have taken the pills and a group who did not, and see if the two groups really lost a significant amount of weight. This is called the experimental method and is a necessary "test" in order to determine the effectiveness or usefulness of a great many things. In many cases, there has been no such research conducted. Ask other questions about why a drug such as this should work and then research whether the claims are plausible and valid. Once your questions receive adequate answers, then you can reach for your credit card.

In terms of your career search, please continue to ask questions. I have had advisees who are set to study a particular major only because their parents want them to. This is unlikely to make for good academic success, and it is more likely to lead to job dissatisfaction one day. Your parents' opinions are useful as part of your decision-making process; after all, they do know you pretty well, but they shouldn't be your only reference. Ask questions and get the answers from books like this or from people working in the field or from solid references such as the *Occupational Outlook Handbook*. Then, arrive at a decision that is yours, not your parents'.

Pay Attention to the Way Terms are Operationalized when Evaluating Information

Operationalizing terms simply means that one clearly defines what might be a fuzzy or ambiguous concept. Honestly, though, it might also be defining what seems to be a clear term. For example, before reading this book you might have tried to determine how long a mental health professional has to go to school or how much money he or she makes. The term "mental health professional" initially may seem like a specific, clear term but you know now after reading this text that that is not true at all. There are many types and levels of mental health professionals, and you have to know to which profession the advice you are receiving applies. That is, to answer your question the term has to be further operationalized.

In scientific research (which you will be reading and digesting in graduate school and beyond), authors must be clear about what exactly they are measuring. An example I often use in my classes to explain this concept concerns research on child day care. The term "day care," on the surface seems to be clear, but it really isn't. Do the researchers mean an institutional or commercial center setting with a number of children and a few select caregivers or do they mean a family setting with one caregiver and just a few children in that caregiver's home or could they be referring to a nanny coming to the child's home where they are one on one with the child or could it even mean a grandparent caring for a child? Additionally, are they studying children who are in one or more of those situations 20 or 40 or 50 hours per week? If you want to research child day care, you need to qualify which of those experiences you are talking about. Because surely the child who is cared for by a nanny for 20 hours per week is having a different experience than the child in an institutional or commercial day care center for 45 hours per week. If you include all of those experiences in your examination as if they are the same thing, your research will not be as valid as someone who looks solely at those children in, say, institutional settings (day care centers) and reports evidence and results as it relates to that setting. When you are reading research about day cares, be sure to see if and how the authors have operationalized the definition.

Can you think of other terms that need to be operationalized? How about aggression? If you are trying to keep track of children's displays of aggression for a project or study you are doing, it is important to operationalize aggression. You would probably believe that it included strong physical contact, such as hitting, punching, or kicking. That would be obvious. However, would it also include pushing past someone? How about raising a hand but not actually hitting? Or would calling someone a mean name be aggressive? How about simply glaring across the playground at someone? It's not that any of these definitions are right or wrong. It's just that you and any co-researchers and those who read the study or hear the project results need to know what you are defining it or operationalizing it as.

Examine the Evidence – Both Sides of the Evidence

One trap we fall into when we are trying to argue a point or take a side is that we prematurely pick a side (sometimes based on emotion) and then only attend to evidence and facts that confirm our opinion instead of being aware of and considering evidence and facts to the contrary. A good example of this is that many Americans identify themselves as Democrat or Republican and then they stand behind or agree with each viewpoint put forth by "their" side without actually studying it. When someone tries to give them arguments for the "other" side, they tune them out and minimize them instead of actually listening and evaluating them. This also happens with many longstanding beliefs. As a frivolous example, you might have been brought up to think that chicken soup cures colds. Every time you get sick you make chicken soup. When I tell you that there is no scientific evidence that chicken soups helps colds, you become insistent and exclaim that you have been using the remedy for years and nothing is going to change your mind. Think about that ... nothing is going to change your mind ... that is the opposite of examining the evidence. Critical thinking means staying open-minded and always being willing to take a look at opposing evidence. That doesn't mean you have to be convinced by that evidence but that you at least consider it.

Some of you may have grown up knowing from a young age that you wanted to work with people to help solve problems related to emotional maladjustment or mental illness. You never even considered a career in business or looked at the pros and cons of being a nurse or found out what physical therapy was all about. When your parents suggested you take a look at these job potentials, you may have responded by saying that nothing was going to change your mind and refused to examine any evidence about other professions. This lack of examination only works against you. As stated before, examining alternatives doesn't mean that evidence will change your mind and that you will then change your major. It does mean that you have critically thought about this important decision. Additionally, you can now explain to your parents exactly why you do not want those jobs and why this profession is more suited to you. So you get to critically think and get your parents to back down.

Analyze Assumptions and Biases of Those Making Claims

When you are trying to evaluate any claim related to research or the virtues of a new product on the market or the desirability of a profession, be sure to examine the assumptions and biases of the individuals making the claim. For example, remember the autism/vaccine controversy conversation earlier in this chapter? Wakefield potentially had outside incentive for arriving at the conclusion he did. There were lawyers helping to fund his research. Those same lawyers had as clients some of the children in Wakefield's study. This does not mean that Wakefield definitely altered any results but the conflict of interest makes it a possibility and makes him biased toward possibly drawing certain conclusions.

Further, I recently had a doctor recommend a new nutritional supplement to me that she has a financial stake in, such that she would profit when people purchase it. Obviously, this might make her more biased about the effectiveness of the supplement. Does she really believe that the supplement works, or is she hoping to increase her income? There are many products out there in which the individuals who give the hardiest endorsement for the product are also selling the product and therefore gaining financially if you make a purchase. Back to my doctor, it could still be a very good supplement that she is recommending. If you trust your doctor, you would hope that she wouldn't recommend something that wasn't effective. Similarly, the product that your friend or acquaintance is using and selling could possibly be effective. It's just that it's now your job to do some research and see whether others (especially scientists who have put the product through experimental research) view these things as effective. Then you can determine if there is indeed any bias on the part of those offering the product.

As far as you making career decisions, consider that in trying to give you information about careers, I made it very clear in my Introduction what my profession was. I did this so you would be aware of any bias that I might have in explaining the differences between professions. Hopefully, I was able to convey useful information without bias, but truly that is part of your job to discern if I did that or not. I have, unfortunately, too often heard others in these mental health professions extol the virtues of their own professions and put down others. It is possible that their critiques of each other are valid. However, you can't know that just by listening to what one biased person has to say. If he or she makes what sounds like a relevant point, go research it more and see if that is indeed correct or if his or her identity in that profession has made him or her biased.

Avoid Emotional Reasoning

One of the starkest examples of working to avoid emotional reasoning is the fact that juries are not made up of people who have any vested interest in the people involved in the crime. Therefore, a mother would not be allowed to sit on a jury for a man accused of molesting her child. The theory here is that her emotions would cloud her judgment of the facts. Further, all mothers who are potential jurors will be carefully vetted and possibly rejected because even though it wasn't HER child that was harmed, as a mother, she may have more emotion and anger at the suspect that could cloud her judgment than someone who does not have children.

Emotional reasoning may impact people's relationships as well. This is something to be aware of for your own life and for the lives of your future clients. We do not reason as well when our emotions are high. There is an old wives' tale that instructs couples to "never go to bed angry." I happen to think that this is not good advice. When arguments start between people (not just couples), the emotion often takes over and no progress is made in making decisions or compromising. After a night of sleep, people typically awaken much calmer. NOW is the time for rational discussion and thinking critically about the problem. Please note that I do believe that the impetus for the argument should not be ignored – just tabled until the individuals involved are calmer and less emotional and better critical thinkers.

In terms of decision-making for your mental health vocation choice, you wouldn't want to let emotions rule your judgment. For example, perhaps you are a math and science whiz and have always wanted to be an engineer. Your parents then go through a divorce during your senior year in high school, which is extremely difficult on you. Therefore, you go to counseling and the therapist helps you tremendously and you decide that now you want to go into the mental health area to give back to others that experienced the kind of pain you went through. Changing your career course for this emotional reason alone is probably ill-advised. Now, if you have had the positive therapy experience and it makes you research the various mental health professions, it spurs you to talk to some people who work in the field, it prompts you to ask questions of your guidance counselor, it makes you compare things like salary, work environment, and job opportunities between mental health professionals and engineers – *then* you will be informed about your choices. Then, you can comfortably change your career trajectory and it won't be based solely on emotion ... which is fleeting.

Consider Other Interpretations

When new pieces of information or facts are disseminated, it is the job of the researchers, the scientists, and, ultimately, the public to draw conclusions about the information. Many times the information that is publicized is absolutely true, but the conclusions we draw are faulty. Let's take a silly example. Here is a fact: every December 25, millions of children across the world wake up to find toys and other presents under a tree in their living room. Now, what conclusion is typically drawn about how this state of affairs comes to pass each year? Obviously, our favorite conclusion is that a kind, jolly, white-bearded, big-bellied old man gets in his sleigh that is pulled by 12 magical reindeer (plus one with a glowing red nose) and makes a stop at the home of EVERY child on the Earth to leave presents and toys that he and his little friends have manufactured in a shop at the North Pole for children who have behaved well that year. Whew. Sounds far-fetched when you hear it spelled out like that, doesn't it? Well, it also begins to sound far-fetched to children as they age and achieve new levels of cognitive development and begin to question and critically think about the world around them. They hear rumblings from peers that there really is no jolly man and that, instead, their parents leave the presents under the tree. Little do those kids (or their parents) know that they have made their first use of Occam's razor. Occam's razor is a scientific and philosophical principle that states that, when there are two competing explanations for a phenomenon, the simplest is most often the correct one. So, bearded man visiting every house in the world with presents or mom and dad secretly giving out gifts to their children. Obviously, the latter is the simpler AND more correct explanation.

Now, this example may seem too simplistic but the principle holds true in so many other situations. For instance, when some people experience vague physical symptoms, such as stomach aches or nausea, it is POSSIBLE that they have stomach cancer. However, it is much more likely that they ate something that didn't agree with them or they have another, much less serious stomach malady. The latter, simpler explanation is more likely true. Further, if a dog owner comes home to find his trash can tipped over and scattered in the kitchen, should he conclude that a robber has broken into his home to look for personal information or that the dog tipped the trash can over? What is more likely, that someone was motivated to choose your home, pick a lock, avoid detection by neighbors, perhaps circumvent a security system, all to take a peek at your personal trash? Or that the dog knocked the can over? The simplest explanation with the fewest number of steps or complications is most often the true conclusion. Keep in mind that Occam's razor does not always hold true. Sometime there are more complicated conclusions. However, it should always be considered when evaluating multiple explanations.

I tell you about Occam's razor because I want you to always consider alternative explanations for phenomena that you encounter. Especially when you are reading about research or other scientific endeavors. Remember Wakefield's conclusion? That his study with 12 children could somehow indict an industry? Was that really the most logical conclusion to draw? Could there have been other reasons why there seemed to be a connection between children receiving vaccinations and children developing autism? Actually, there is. The simpler explanation has to do more with timing. The MMR vaccines are typically delivered when the child is in the early toddler years. Autism is also first identifiable at about that time. The simpler explanation is that the two things simply occur together, not that one is causing the other. Correlation does not imply causation. If that phrase is not familiar to you, Google it and see why it is so important in research and in the mental health field.

Tolerate Uncertainty

In this age of technology and having instant access to information, we often feel like there should be an answer for everything. However, there often either isn't an answer yet, or the answer we have is really tentative until we find a better answer, or perhaps there will never be an answer! It can be uncomfortable when we do not know the answer for sure, and we therefore strive to keep finding the answer. That is fine. Critical thinkers keep striving. And critical thinkers will not prematurely settle on something because they realize that what we are very sure about today may be turned upside down tomorrow. Remember the example from Galileo's time about whether the Earth was the center of the universe? They thought they had the puzzle figured out but new information came to light – and many non-critical thinkers couldn't be dissuaded by that new information.

Uncertainty is destined to exist because sometimes there is more than one answer for a problem and that unexpected reality has clouded our judgment. For example, we all know that cancer has more than one cause. Not only are there are multiple causes for each kind of cancer but, even if we isolate just one type of cancer, say lung cancer, there are still multiple causes for it (genetics, smoking, environmental factors). Additionally, we may be uncertain about the specific cause for any one person. Most of us readily believe and understand this uncertainty, but if we apply the same paradigm to something like alcohol and drug addiction we are more skeptical. Just like with the causes of cancer, there are actually several theories about why someone succumbs to addictive disorders. That is, why do some people use drugs and become addicted and others use them and do not become addicted and others never even try them in the first place? The truth is that we still may not know exactly what causes these differences. It may be something that we discover after more research. Or perhaps there really isn't ONE cause but various people abuse substances for various reasons. Despite all this, there will be plenty of (non-critical thinking) people who cannot tolerate this uncertainty and insist that their particular theory applies to most every addict. Uncertainty is a fact of life.

Tolerating uncertainty also means that guidelines and rules may change as we learn more about a particular topic. For example, you may or may not know that doctors and nurses used to recommend that parents put their newborn babies to sleep on their tummies. The theory was that if they spit up or vomited they would not choke on it. Then, more research was done on a phenomena termed SIDS – sudden infant death syndrome. (Google more about this heartbreaking event if you haven't heard of it.) Briefly, it involves the death of a seemingly healthy infant, usually during sleep. At this point we do not know the cause of SIDS. The cause is uncertain. However, we do know that babies who sleep on their stomachs are more likely to die from it. Therefore, doctors and nurses have changed their recommendation and now urge parents to places their babies on their backs or sides to sleep. Guidelines changed. It is possible that this recommendation could change again if new information comes to light. Uncertainty is a fact of life.

In regard to your career choice, uncertainty is a fact of life. All you can do is collect the most information possible, ask trusted resources their opinions, and make an informed decision. Then you should realize that new information may come to light and it may make you consider changing your mind. That's ok. Critical thinkers tolerate uncertainty.

In summary, the critical thinking principle detailed above will help you to effectively and efficiently navigate the massive amounts of information that you come into contact with in your personal and professional life. Beware of psychobabble and ask questions. When examining evidence related to both personal and professional issues, take note of how terms are defined, always examine evidence on both sides of an issue while realizing that uncertainty about some issues is inevitable. Finally, understand that bias can affect the judgment of people, as can strong emotions.

References

Flaherty, D. K. (2011). The vaccine-autism connection: A public health crisis caused by unethical medical practices and fraudulent science. *Annals of Pharmacotherapy*, 45(10), 1302–1304.

Madsen, K. M., Hviid, A., Vetergaard, M., Schendel, D., Wohlfahrt, J., Thorsen, P., Olsen J., & Melbye, M. (2002). A population-based study of measles, mumps, and rubella vaccination and autism. *New England Journal of Medicine*, 347(19), 1477–1482.

Marwick, C. (2001). U.S. report finds no link between MMR and autism. *British Medical Journal*, 322(7294), 1083.

Occupational outlook handbook (2014–15 ed.). Washington, DC: Bureau of Labor Statistics, U.S. Department of Labor.

Taylor, L. E., Swerdfeger, A. L., & Eslick, G.D. (2014). Vaccines are not associated with autism: An evidence-based meta-analysis of case-control and cohort studies. *Vaccine*, 32(29), 3623–3629.

Wade, C., & Tavris, C. (2014). *Invitation to psychology*. New York: Pearson.

Wakefield, A. E., Murch, M. B, Anthony, A., Linnell, J., Casson, D. M., Malik, M., Berelowitz, M., Dhillon, A. P., Thomson, M. A., Harvey, P., Valentine, A., Davies, S. E., & Walker-Smith, J. A. (1998). Ileal-lymphoid-nodular hyperplasia, non-specific colitis, and pervasive development disorder in children. *The Lancet*, 351(9103), 637–641.

10

Ethics: A Primer on Mental Health Profession Guidelines

Once you are accepted and begin graduate school, you will learn a great deal about ethics and professionalism. However, I believe it is useful to give you a brief primer here about some of the ethical guidelines that you will be expected to uphold in an effort to provide a taste of the implications of being a mental health professional. Each mental health profession will adhere to its own set of ethical standards. For example, psychologists follow the *Ethical Principles of Psychologists and Code of Conduct* (American Psychological Association, 2010) and mental health counselors follow the *American Counseling Association Code of Ethics* (American Counseling Association, 2014) while social workers adhere to the *NASW Code of Ethics* (National Association of Social Workers, 2009) and marriage and family therapists use the *AAMFT Code of Ethics* (American Association of Marriage and Family Therapy, 2015). Further, the *NAADAC Ethical Standards of Alcoholism and Drug Addiction Counselors* (National Association of Addiction Professionals, 2011) is used by substance abuse counselors. There is even a more generic *Ethical Standards for Human Service Professionals* (National Organization for Human Services, 2015). While each profession has its own code, as you might guess, there is a great deal of overlap and commonality between them. This chapter will *by no means* be an extensive or thorough treatment of ethical issues. I just want to comment on some of the ethical commonalities between the

Careers in Mental Health: Opportunities in Psychology, Counseling, and Social Work,
First Edition. Kim Metz.

occupations and how they can impact mental health professionals. Therefore, let's take a brief look at some of the most important parts of any of the ethics codes – those that relate to issues of confidentiality, boundaries, and record-keeping.

Confidentiality

Confidentiality is likely not a new term for you. You may have heard of HIPAA (Health Insurance Portability and Accountability Act), which, among other things, safeguards your medical records and assures that their security and confidentiality will be protected. There is also a confidentiality rule in higher education titled FERPA (Family Educational Rights and Privacy Act) that dictates who can see your academic records from college. In mental health the confidentiality concerns who has access to your mental health records and to whom the information can be disclosed. This may seem pretty simple. Of course you would not give out client records to just anyone who asks. However, there are many nuances to this. For example, just the fact that a client is being seen at all is considered a confidential piece of information that you may not reveal unless the client gives you permission. As I mentioned, you will go over these types of technical aspects during your training. What I would like to highlight is the real-world implications to this rule that are important to consider if you are considering a career in a mental health profession.

First, depending on the size of town that you live and work in, you may come across people whom you have seen or are seeing in therapy. For example, a client could be a parent of a player at your daughter's volleyball game. Or perhaps you just discovered that one of the kids on your son's new baseball team was a past client. Because their professional interaction with you is confidential, being able to navigate these kinds of encounters are part of maintaining that confidentiality. This is especially true because clients will have different ideas of how they feel the situation should be handled. Remember, it's *their* confidentiality. Some clients will appreciate discretion and others will not care if people are aware of their therapy status. For example, while shopping in a department store years ago, a female 20-something-year-old client bounded up to me, dragging her mother with her, and happily exclaimed in the middle of the women's clothing section that I was her therapist. Obviously, this is not the norm when you run into someone in public, but part of the issue is that there really is no norm. My general rule of thumb is that if I see a client at a location outside of the therapy office, I let them make the first move and, until they do, act as if I don't know them. Oh – and lest you think you will be immune from such concerns because you plan to make sure that you work in a different city than where you live – know that I live in Ohio and that several years ago I ran into a client of mine while I was on a spring break with my family in a gift shop in Florida!

Another real-life type of confidentiality situation can occur when you have a client who is high-profile in some way. Now, most of you will likely not be conducting marriage counseling with Brad and Angelina, but there are other ways for a client to be high-profile. For example, local politicians or civic leaders may have personal or family issues they are trying to resolve in therapy. When you see that community leader in the news or campaigning for a position, you must continue to keep his or her client status confidential even years after your professional contact. Perhaps you counsel a teacher at the local high school; this could be considered high profile in your community and would obviously be something you could not share with others. Further, there may be someone who becomes high-profile because he or she has broken the law and possibly even made the news. While you may be tempted to talk to others about how you saw that person in therapy last year, you must still maintain confidentiality. High-profile can also just mean that the person is unique enough in the community that he or she is easily identifiable. For example, you may think that you are safe telling your lunch mate about your new client who has recently become a millionaire through a family inheritance, because you do not divulge the person's name. However, that description may be enough for your lunch mate (or even the people sitting in the booth next to you) to easily guess who the client is, thereby compromising the client's confidentiality.

Of course, there are some limits to confidentiality. You will explore the nuances of these limits much more during your graduate training. However, it is worthwhile to take a brief look at those limits now. First, if a client is a danger to himself or herself, you, as the therapist, are allowed and expected to report this danger. A client who is actively suicidal cannot just be sent home. While you will learn the specifics later, there are ways to assess for suicide risk. Briefly, you want to know that the client has the intent, that he or she has a plan, and that they have the means or could easily acquire the means to act on the plan. If the client has attempted suicide in the past, that will increase his or her current risk. If, after assessing the client, you reasonably expect that he or she is at risk for self-harm, you may have to confide that information to a parent or to a spouse of your client, you may have to call the police who could transport the client to an appropriate place, or it may be that you have to call medical personnel directly in order to get the person to the hospital as soon as possible.

A second reason that confidentiality can be broken is if the client is a danger to someone else. Google "Tarasoff" or "duty to warn" and read in detail about the groundbreaking case in this area. Briefly, it involved a client named Tatiana Tarasoff from California who was murdered by a man who was in therapy. The man had disclosed his intentions to his therapist who did make some moves to warn someone, campus police, of the client's intention. Believing him not to be a threat, he was released. Several months later he did indeed kill Ms. Tarasoff. Her family sued because they were not warned of the man's intentions. Initially, the court found that the therapist did have a "duty to warn" the intended victim, but a higher court determined that a "duty to protect" was called for. That is, the therapist must take whatever steps necessary to protect the intended victim (e.g., telling the victim, telling the family of the victim, telling the police, or by whatever other means necessary). This is obviously important to all of the mental health codes, since it involves breaking the confidentiality of the therapist/client relationship. The implications of this ruling reach beyond just explicit threats of violence. This ruling can impact how a therapist deals with a client who has AIDS or is HIV-positive and is engaging in sexual activity with someone who is unaware of your client's diagnosis. It may come into play when working with a domestic violence victim and perpetrator in couple counseling. It is an area that will be discussed and dissected in your training.

Another reason that confidentiality may be broken is if a therapist knows or suspects that a child or an elderly person or a person with disabilities is being physically or sexually abused or neglected. This is actually a duty that other professionals, such as doctors and teachers, also have a responsibility to act upon. We call those individuals "mandated reporters." Depending upon the agency in which you work, this situation may occur more or less often. In my 20 years of working in community mental health and private practice, there have only been a handful of times that I was presented with a situation such as this. However, if you work as a social worker in a child welfare office, you will likely have to contend more often with this; or, if your practice is primarily with children and adolescents, you may have more cause to encounter such situations. Let me add here that I had a student who wanted to work in mental health but, when she learned that reporting abuse might be an eventuality, she changed her mind saying that it would be too stressful to have that responsibility. If you have the qualities to be a good mental health professional, realize that your training will help you become versed in how to cope with and handle these types of conflictual situations.

A final reason that confidentiality will not be maintained has to do with outside parties who may be able to become privy to parts of your work with a client. The first outside party would be insurance companies. In order to get reimbursed for treatment, you will have to report a client's diagnosis to the company. Some companies will want periodic updates or treatment plans to aid in their deciding whether the therapy is covered. The second outside party that may have access to your treatment records may be the courts. For a variety of reasons the court may produce an order requiring you to turn over records or even testify in court about specifics related to your client. For example, if parents are in a custody dispute, the court may request records of your treatment with their child to help make a judgment about custody or some aspect of custody. Alternatively, the court may request the therapy records of someone who has faced criminal charges, perhaps for substance use, in an effort to determine if the client is following through on the court's requirements, such as regular therapy sessions or abstinence from drugs and alcohol.

Boundaries

Another ethical principle shared by most mental health professionals is related to maintaining boundaries between you and your client. One example of this is engaging in *multiple relationships* – also called *dual relationships*, or, in the mental health counselor nomenclature, *counselor–client non-professional relationships.* This occurs when you are in a professional relationship with the client but then also engage in another type of relationship with that client. The most egregious way to do this would be to engage in a sexual relationship. I always think this is such an obvious breach of ethics, but it is violated by therapists so it is worth discussing briefly. One of the reasons for keeping clear boundaries with a client is because the nature of the client/therapist relationship is that the therapist is always in a "one-up" position over the client. To explain, consider that most relationships are based on reciprocity. That is, there is a mutual exchange of information between the individuals. In a therapeutic relationship, there is no mutual exchange. Therapists do not share their emotions or personal experiences, nor do they share details about, for example, their childhood or the state of their marriage or their dissatisfaction with their job. This means that the therapist will always know much more about the client than the client will ever know about the therapist. Hence the idea that the therapist is always one-up on the client. This status is acceptable and necessary for professional connection but, if the therapist tries to make the relationship more personal, he/she now has an unfair advantage. The client is in a more vulnerable position and a situation is created in which manipulation and exploitation, even unintentional, of the client is possible because the therapist is aware of so many of the client's inner feelings, anxieties and weaknesses. In addition to the "one-up" issue, consider that many clients may be seeing a therapist because they have issues with trust or boundaries. Obviously, engaging in a sexual relationship with this more vulnerable person will do little to help the client with these types of problems.

There are other seemingly more innocent ways to violate this ethical principle of maintaining boundaries. Seeing a client who is a friend or seeing a relative of a good friend is an example of a multiple relationship. Additionally, engaging in a business relationship before or after seeing the client in therapy constitutes a dual relationship, as does selling your car to a client or borrowing money from a client or being a guest at a client's wedding or graduation. The APA code of ethics defines multiple relationships, forbids sexual ones, and recommends that a therapist avoid any dual relationship that can potentially "impair the psychologist's objectivity, competence or effectiveness in performing his or her functions as a psychologist, or otherwise risks exploitation or harm to the person with whom the professional relationship exists" (American Psychological Association, 2010).

Incidentally, in the way that the code is written (and the way that the counselor code is written) there is room for the therapist to determine if a dual relationship will be detrimental to the client. For example, accepting a client's invitation to his/her high school graduation probably poses little risk to the client, while engaging in a financial transaction such as buying or selling a car to the client may impair the therapist's objectivity. Additionally, there may be situations in which a dual relationship is not detrimental and may even be necessary. For example, in smaller towns there may not be many choices of therapists, so a person may engage in therapy with someone with whom he or she has had personal contact. Further, in poorer rural areas, therapy may be bartered for a good or service that the client can provide, such as farm produce or assistance with painting a home. It is important to think critically about such situations before engaging in them. It is also important to document your reasoning and perhaps consult with a colleague to be sure your decision-making ability is not clouded.

While not explicitly discussed in most of the ethics codes, boundary issues may bleed into your personal life as well. These issues could also come under the heading of professionalism. The basic idea is that you want to conduct yourself in personal matters in ways that would not be unbecoming of a therapist or helping profession. For example, while it is perfectly acceptable to have a night out on the weekend, you would want to refrain from being inebriated in public lest one of your clients frequent the same establishment. It would undermine your competence for them to see you in such a state. Further, consider the information that you might make public on social media. If such information is accessible to your clients, you would want to be careful what you post and/or tweet. I'm sure you have by now had all the privacy and social media lectures from your parents and teachers. Their advice will still be useful when you are a professional adult. The most obvious potential problem is posting too much of your personal life – in pictures, posts or tweets – for others to view. Again, just like mom and your English teacher tried to tell you! However, you should monitor not only the types of pictures you post but also the updates you provide to your "friends." For example, you may not want your politics or religious preference to be available for clients to view in the form of posts you make or like or share, as it may color their attitude about you as their clinician or make them feel that you might not be open to hearing certain issues that they have. It's not that you can't have your own opinions or values, but you don't want those things to get in the way of a client feeling that he or she can talk to you without judgment.

Record-Keeping

Another part of most ethical codes concerns the importance of record-keeping. Mental health professionals have to create, maintain, store, and eventually destroy files on each client. Each agency you work for will have its own policies and procedures for accomplishing this. What you must be aware of is that documentation is important, and you must attend to the detail involved in the processing of it. It can include, among other things, anything from treatment plans, progress notes, test results, reports or evaluations, past client records, school records, consent for treatment, and personal information. Record maintenance is important for several reasons. First, progress notes that you complete at the end of every session help remind you what goals were worked on and what should be accomplished in subsequent sessions. Accurate record-keeping also can be necessary in case your client chooses to release them to another professional who may treat the client concurrently or in the future. Records are also needed in order to receive payment from many insurance companies. These third-party payers may review your records to ensure that the services they are paying for are being conducted by you. At times they may request updates to a client's treatment plan in order to gauge their progress. This state of affairs is often lamented by treatment providers as they dislike a third party (who may or may not be another mental health professional) having purview over their client's treatment. While I actually share this concern, at this time there are mandates set forth by the third-party payers that must be followed if you want to receive reimbursement for your services. A final reason to keep good records would be to allow the possibility for another clinician to replicate successful work that you have done with someone. To take this even further, perhaps you may want to conduct research on how well a particular approach has worked on a particular type of client.

As stated, much of your education about record-keeping will come from the agency within which you work. But there are a few tips that I can give you that will be useful wherever you work. For example, always complete records at work rather than taking them home with you. If you work in a place where face-to-face interactions with clients are intense and continual, you may feel like there is not time to do paper-work on the job. Find a way to do it! Most agencies will have policies about such a thing because removing records or charts can cause problems. What if another treatment professional in the facility needs access to the record? Or what if you have a car accident or your car is stolen with files in the car? Confidentiality could easily be compromised or the record itself could be destroyed. A more personal reason is that waiting for the end of the day to record-keep really will add a substantial amount of time to your day. When I began doing outpatient counseling I would often wait until the end of the day to complete my progress notes because I felt like I had to get the next client into session to keep my hourly appointments on track. However, it added unpaid time to my day, and it was more difficult to remember exactly what happened during a session that occurred 7 hours ago. My practice now is to write notes partially during the session and completely by the end of a session before my next client. In outpatient therapy a typical "session" is about 50 minutes according to most insurance companies. You should strive to maintain the 50-minute hour so that you have 10 minutes to thoroughly complete your documentation.

It should be noted that medical record-keeping in general has under-gone significant changes with the advances in technology. Many more agencies and facilities use some form of computer-based treatment documentation. Again, the nuances of this will be something covered by the agency where you are employed. Be aware that issues of confidentiality and being sure that others cannot gain access to the computerized record will be of the utmost importance. This is also paramount when you consider that confidential information can also be sent across text messages and emails. Ensuring the integrity of these media is a necessity.

References

American Association for Marriage and Family Therapy (2015). *AAMFT code of ethics*. Alexandria, VA: American Association for Marriage and Family Therapy.

American Counseling Association (2014). *ACA code of ethics*. Alexandria, VA: American Counseling Association.

American Psychological Association (2010). *Ethical principles of psychologists and code of conduct*. Washington, DC: American Psychological Association.

National Association of Addiction Professionals (2011). *NAADAC ethical standards of alcoholism and drug addiction counselors*. Alexandria, VA: National Association of Addiction Professionals.

National Association of Social Workers. (2009). *NASW code of ethics*. Washington, DC. NASW Press.

National Organization for Human Services (2015). *Ethical standards for human services professionals*. Melbourne, FL: National Organization for Human Services.

11

How to Increase Your Chance of Getting into Graduate School

You should by now have a better idea if this area of study and eventual career is really for you. If you decide that it is, here are a few hints that will aid you in your application process for graduate school. Remember that some graduate programs are more difficult to get accepted than others. For example, clinical Ph.D. psychology programs have more rigorous standards, will have more individuals apply, and will accept fewer students than the other programs that were discussed in Unit 1. Therefore, these tips are especially helpful for those attempting to be admitted into more competitive programs. However, competencies in each of these areas will be helpful no matter which type of program you are choosing. When you are exploring various graduate programs, also keep in mind that they will all have different policies related to financial aid. For example, if you are trying to pursue a Ph.D. in clinical or counseling psychology, so few applicants are accepted that the school will often waive tuition provided that the graduate student performs a service such as teach a class or be an assistant to a full-time professor. Schools in other disciplines will often not be able to offer as much financial incentive, but there will usually be some opportunities to lower the bottom-line tuition dollar. Some schools offer classes primarily in the evening so that you can hold a full-time job during the day. Others will expect that you dedicate your time to school versus work. As you examine graduate schools, note their financial aid incentives.

Careers in Mental Health: Opportunities in Psychology, Counseling, and Social Work,
First Edition. Kim Metz.

Once ready to apply, the following are things that the graduate school will likely be using to evaluate your application.

GPA and GRE Scores

Graduate schools will generally place a great deal of importance on your grade-point average and on your score on the Graduate Record Examination (GRE) (or perhaps the Miller Analogies Test (MAT) depending on the school). Your grade-point average (GPA) and standardized test scores are sometimes used as the first cutoff in the application process. Think of them as necessary but not sufficient for getting into graduate schools; that is, a high number will keep you in the running but won't ensure your acceptance. For many master's programs a minimum 3.0 GPA is used as a cutoff. If your GPA is high enough, some master's level program schools may not require a GRE score. Others may require both. If you are applying to a Ph.D. program, the minimum GPA will be higher – usually above a 3.5. Whatever program you are considering, check out the school's website and there will typically be a link that includes statistics about its incoming class for the last few years. Check to see how your numbers compare with those of the most recent incoming classes to help you determine if you have a realistic chance of being accepted.

If your GPA is not stellar, one thing to try to do is highlight any improvement made during your later undergraduate years. Perhaps freshman year was too much fun, but you wised up by sophomore year and improved your grades. Try to include information in your application that highlights the average of your last six semesters versus eight. If your GPA is not close to a 3.5 cutoff, then you may do well to consider master's degree programs at least as back-ups to your dream graduate school.

The most common standardized tests used are the GRE and the MAT. The GRE General Test is a test much like the SAT that you may have taken to get into college. It measures verbal reasoning, quantitative reasoning, and analytic writing. The entire test takes 3 hours and 45 minutes, and is broken up into 6 sections with a break halfway through. The test is now offered at over 1,000 test centers in over 160 countries. It can be taken on a computer at those locations. To sign up for a time to take the exam, you must go to the GRE website and search for a location near you and then search for seat availability at that location. Be sure to attend to when your test results will be available so that they can be delivered to your graduate school selections by their deadlines. Despite being a computer-based exam, test takers do have the ability to skip questions and go back within a section. The GRE also offers subject tests in various areas, and there is a psychology subject test that attempts to measure your basic knowledge of psychology. However, not every graduate school requires that the subject test be taken. Be sure to check what your choices of schools desire. You do not want to waste time and money taking the subject test if it isn't needed.

As you may remember from taking the SAT, there is no shortage of books to buy, websites to visit, and classes to take to try to improve your score on the GRE. It is an important number looked at by admission committees, so as soon as you know that you are interested in graduate school begin researching the exam and taking practice tests. Get a sense of the score you are likely to earn and compare it with what an incoming first-year graduate student at your top-choice schools earn.

Research the schools you are most interested in because some may prefer you to take the MAT. If so, you obviously want to spend more time studying and practicing it. It is a 60-minute test made up of 120 analogies (A is to B as C is to D). It measures your ability to recognize relationships between ideas as well as your general knowledge in math, science, humanities, and social science. Again, the best way to practice for it is going to be to take as many free sample tests as you can.

Research Experience

This section is more important if you are applying to a doctoral (Ph.D.) program, but it will bolster your application for master's programs as well. Though most of you may not desire to conduct much research during your career, it is still imperative that you are able to understand and digest scientific research. We must do this so that we can stay up to date on the most recent and effective methods in the field. If you are planning on a doctoral degree, you will be expected to conduct original research. Indeed, being able to conduct that research yourself is an invaluable way to truly understand and critically evaluate the research of others.

You can be involved in research in a couple of ways. First, as an undergraduate you can connect with a faculty member who is doing his/her own research and try to join his/her research team. You could potentially be a part of designing the research, collecting or analyzing the data, or writing the conclusions. If there is not this opportunity at your college, you can also always work on completing your own research. There is a vast amount of things you could scientifically explore. I regularly mention to students in my classes that "this" or "that" topic is prime for further research. Most undergraduate programs will encourage you to accomplish such a project. Typically, a faculty member will oversee your project. Ask if there is a way to earn academic credit for your work. Many schools will also find a way to showcase the research work of undergraduate students in a type of mini-conference. If your school does this, take advantage and present your results. It will give you experience talking to peers and faculty about your research, and you will perhaps get some constructive feedback on your project. If you can present at a local, regional, or even a national conference, this will be even more advantageous for you to include in your application. If you can get your research results published, this holds even more weight for an admissions committee.

Volunteering

It's in your best interest to engage in some kind of volunteer work in the mental health area while you are an undergraduate. This is something that may show an admissions committee that you have explored the field to some degree and are still sure that you want to continue your education in this area. More importantly, volunteer work (or paid work, if you can get it) will help YOU see that you truly enjoy working with people. Do this early in your undergraduate career so that, if you find that it isn't something you enjoy, you have time to pursue other education options. Places to volunteer will vary based on where you live and what your interests are. Most communities or nearby communities will have at least some of the following sites: crisis (or suicide) hotlines, battered women's shelters, nursing homes, summer camps, rape crisis centers, an agency that works with disabled children or adults, Big Brothers/Big Sisters, Special

Olympics, homeless shelters, or Habitat for Humanity. I'm sure you can think of many others near your home or school.

Internships

Some undergraduate social science programs may offer the opportunity to complete an internship in a mental health placement. If they offer this option, it would be beneficial to obtain an internship. However, keep in mind that this will not usually be the most important thing looked at by admission committees. This is mostly due to the fact that, since you are only an undergraduate, you will not have the proper training yet, nor will you possess a license to practice; therefore, you will have limited duties wherever you are placed. However, an internship is going to give you exposure to the field and to professionals who work in the field. You will be able to use your experience to help explain to admissions committees why you are drawn to mental health work. You will typically have a supervisor at your internship site who is probably not connected to your university. This could easily be a person who could write a letter of recommendation for you and be able to speak about your professional, leadership, and interpersonal skills first hand. As stated earlier, it is unlikely that your experience on an internship will outweigh things like your GPA and standardized test scores, but it can only help your overall application as well as solidify your desire to work in a mental health profession.

Personal Statement

Many graduate schools will request that you write an essay that some will term a "personal statement." This letter is the admissions committee's way to get to know a little bit about you and, more importantly, your career goals. Sometimes schools will request a general letter and sometimes they will ask specific questions. Be sure to pay attention to exactly what each school is requesting. You should take pains to not just send the same essay to every program, but to modify it based on the specifics of each program. If you are asked for a more general statement, you will undoubtedly be unsure what to include. If you Google "how to write a personal statement" you will find a great deal of useful advice. You might be familiar with Purdue OWL. It is a website hosted by Purdue University that describes and illustrates how to properly do a great deal of scientific and technical writing. Among other things, it can give you good information about writing using APA style. Moreover, the following link from Purdue OWL, https://owl.english. purdue.edu/owl/resource/642/01/, also gives you good information about what to include in a personal statement.

In brief, I will mention just a few things that it recommends. First, try to construct your opening paragraph such that it will catch the attention of admissions committee members who will read a large number of personal statements each year or each semester. It also stresses that you should do some research on the school and the faculty in the program in which you are interested. Find things that are going on at the school or within the department in which you might want to become involved. Show that you are a good fit at the school and in the program. Further, determine the research interests of faculty in the department and note which of them you might be interested in working with and why. Often graduate students have mentor-type relationships with professors and it is, therefore, advantageous to identify which professor you see yourself working with. Finally, be sure that your writing is spell-checked and grammatically correct. Ask several people to proofread it for you. You do not want to give the impression to the admissions committee that you put together your application hastily.

In terms of what kind of information to include, talk about why you are interested in the mental health field and what kinds of experiences you have had that have helped you remained committed. Having said that, I would not recommend including too much information about personal trauma or difficulties that you have experienced. Many students do enter the field for such reasons but, by the time you are graduating from college, you should have other motives that you came by more intentionally for pursuing this career option. In your personal statement you could, therefore, talk about specific things that you have learned in school and how they have helped solidify your choice of career. Try to avoid clichés about wanting to "help people" or "work with children." There are myriad careers that involve both of those things. Be sure to explain why you are choosing to try to accomplish these things via a mental health career versus some other avenue.

Letters of Recommendation

Graduate schools will undoubtedly ask for letters of recommendation to be included with your application. These letters will help the admissions committee see how your professors view your potential to thrive and succeed in graduate school. In order to get good letters of recommendation you need to do a few things.

First, get to know your professors and let them get to know you. Begin this early, as early as freshman year. Most professors will have office hours during which time they make themselves available to students for questions or just to interact. You do not have to go to them daily or even weekly but, a few times a semester, stop in and talk with your professors or advisors. Ask them a question concerning class or about advising or their own career path. Share a few specifics about your classes or your career goals or a struggle and how you are working to overcome it. The more that a few professors or advisors know about you, the more detailed letter they will be able to write about you one day.

Second, make sure that the things your professors know or learn about you are positive. You will have these teachers in class and they will learn a lot (probably the most) about you from your participation and performance in those classes. Be sure that they view you as a good student. You want them to see you as someone who attends class regularly, asks thoughtful questions, offers appropriate comments during class, works well in a team, demonstrates critical thinking, performs well on tests and other assignments, and meets deadlines without complaint.

Third, try to find other ways to interact with faculty. Join a club they advise. If possible, ask if you can work on their research team. If that opportunity doesn't exist, see if a professor will agree to supervise you conducting your own research. The more contexts in which they know you, the better your professors can accurately (and hopefully positively) characterize you in a letter of recommendation.

Fourth, when you make your request for a letter, give them ample time to write a good one. You should be aware of all deadlines, so give them 4–6 weeks to complete the letter and send a reminder in the form of an email 2–3 weeks before your deadline. Additionally, be aware that some faculty may not feel like they know you well enough or that they can write a positive enough letter for you and will, therefore, decline writing one. If that occurs, ensure there is enough time remaining to request a letter from someone else.

Fifth, give each of them a packet of additional information to help their letters be more complete. This is especially true if you feel a professor does not know you that well. Some things to include would be a current resume, a list of classes that you have taken over your undergraduate career with that professor, the grade that you receive in each class, a list of schools that you are applying to, the deadline for each school, and preaddressed and stamped envelopes. Many schools have now gone to online services in order to collect letters so the envelope and stamps may not always be necessary.

Sixth, each school will ask whether you want to be able to view the letter or whether you will waive your right to see it. Be sure to waive your right to view it. Many students have a tendency to think it best to read the letter because they want to see what has been written. However, resist the temptation. To the graduate school it will appear as if you were unsure if the letter would be good and then perhaps refrained from submitting less-than-stellar ones. The graduate school needs to be sure that the recommender feels free to be as open and honest about the candidate as possible. They may doubt that will be the case if the recommender thinks the candidate will read the letter. If you are not sure if your professors will pen a positive letter, ask them. Instead of just asking them to write for you, ask them if they are able to write a positive letter for you. Most professors will be honest and say that they can't write a recommendation for you because it won't be very positive or because they don't feel that they know you well enough to compose a thorough one. This is why my first few points of getting to know a few faculty outside of the classroom early in your college career, while still performing well in their classes, is important.

Vita or Resume

Your graduate application will likely call for some description of your accomplishments and activities achieved thus far in your college career. Some schools may want this listed in a resume, while others may request a curriculum vita or vitae – also often called a CV. The difference between a resume and a CV is, first, that a resume is shorter, typically one page and the CV is lengthier, typically three or four pages. The biggest content-related difference is that a resume highlights your professional or employment experience, while a CV reflects your academic identity. There is really no standard format for a CV, just as there isn't really a standard format for a resume. However, you can include on a CV your relevant research experience as well as academic classes you have taken. When it comes time to write either document, research some possible formats and then ask peers or a professor or two to proofread and critique it.

Interview

Some graduate programs may conduct an in-person interview. If you are invited to one, this is a good sign. Be sure to prepare so that you leave the admissions committee with a good impression. Streufert (2015) gives some useful advice for navigating graduate school interviews. For example, just as in your personal statement, you want to make sure that your interviewers understand that you know something about the school and program to which you are applying. So research these things and try to explain how you see yourself fitting into their school. Further, before the interview, consider the "typical" questions and how you might answer them (strengths, weaknesses, most recent book read). One of the first requests they will likely make of you is to "tell us about yourself." Rehearse your answer to a question such as this. While you want to include a brief amount of personal information, use the opportunity more to illustrate how much your interests match the focus of their program. You will also want to be sure to explain how you have come to the decision to pursue a mental health degree. As Streufert (2015) stresses, don't talk about wanting to help people or about your own mental health struggles. While those things may be your initial reason for studying in the field, you should have engaged in activities during college that solidified those initial reasons. These are the types of things to share in an interview. Another thing to keep in mind is that you may have contact with support staff, current graduate students, or other school administrators. They are informally interviewing you as well and will likely be asked their opinion of you. Finally, be sure to follow up with a thank you to the people involved in your interview process.

Attend to Deadlines

Be sure to understand all of the deadlines required for your chosen program/s. If you are applying to a Ph.D. program, deadlines will likely be in the Fall of your senior year. Typically those programs only accept students for Fall of the following year. It is the same with some master's level programs, but you will also find some that practice a "rolling admissions" process. This means that you can apply anytime and their committee will review your application as it arrives. If accepted for admission, you would be eligible to begin at the start of the next semester. Each school's website is likely to have its deadlines clearly delineated. The difficult part may be to keep track of who wants what when. I recommend that you design some kind of spreadsheet that can help you track your progress with each program in which you are interested.

There is another thing related to deadlines. That is, depending on which program you are applying to, applications may be due anywhere from November of your senior year up through the summer after your senior year. If you are applying somewhere with an early deadline, then you want to be sure you have accomplished some of the aforementioned things before that time. Consider that, if you are doing an internship during the last semester of your senior year, you will not really be able to talk about it in an application that is due in your first semester of your senior year. Similarly, if you can get involved with research, try to do it early enough in your undergraduate career so you can complete a project (on your own or with a team) and present the results at some type of professional conference before your senior year.

Reference

Streufert, B. (2015). How to ace your grad school interview. *USA Today*. Retrieved from http://college.usatoday.com/2015/02/20/how-to-ace-your-grad-school-interview/

12

After You Have Earned Your Degree

Thus far in this unit, you have examined some of your motivations to work in the mental health field and have considered some of the ethical guidelines and critical thinking skills that will be significant for you. Let's assume that you follow the suggestions for how to get into graduate school and get accepted, graduate, and licensed. This chapter is a short list of things you will encounter or have to contend with.

Continuing Education

No matter which route you choose in the mental health field, you will be responsible for continuing to learn about your discipline long after completing graduate school. This is referred to as continuing education and is actually a requirement for a great many professions outside the mental health field as well (e.g., teachers, lawyers) that have some kind of licensure involved with their profession. Not following through with the required number of continuing education hours could cause you to lose your license. It is also another area in which the requirements are going to vary from profession to profession and from state to state. Whichever mental health profession you choose to pursue, you will need to go to the corresponding state licensing board to determine exactly what continuing education is required of you.

Careers in Mental Health: Opportunities in Psychology, Counseling, and Social Work,
First Edition. Kim Metz.
© 2016 John Wiley & Sons, Ltd. Published 2016 by John Wiley & Sons, Ltd.

Typically, license renewal will happen every 2 years. During the ensuing 2 years, professionals will take classes related to their discipline for a prescribed number of hours. It would be too lengthy to list every state's requirement for each profession but, to give you some idea, the rule for psychologists in Ohio is 23 hours of continuing education every 2 years. Three of those hours must be in the area of ethics. Mental health counselors, social workers, and marriage and family therapists in Ohio are required to participate in 30 hours of continuing education every 2 years, with 3 of those hours in the area of ethics.

The continuing education courses can be taken in person in a traditional classroom format. Various providers will be approved by the state licensing board and will offer classes on a variety of topics in cities throughout the United States. There are also now online opportunities to engage in continuing education hours. Each licensing board will have rules regarding the number of online hours that may count toward your total.

Continuing education hours are essential for a few reasons. First, the mental health field is constantly changing as new research is conducted and published and new theories formed. While you are in graduate school you are learning about cutting-edge information and techniques. Five to 10 or 20 years later you will still have access to the current literature by keeping up with professional journals in your field; however, many professionals do not do this due to time constraints. The mandate for continuing education ensures that you keep up with at least some current practices in the field. Second, many mental health professionals will find that they desire to create a "niche" for themselves. Perhaps they want to specialize in attention deficit disorder or marital infidelity or eating disorders. Continuing education can help you hone an area or discover an area in which you want to have specialized training. Finally, attending continuing education is a way to network with other professionals with similar interests. This networking can help you discover the best practices that your colleagues might be using with their clients. It can also be beneficial in trying to gauge what types of employment opportunities your colleagues have found and, if you are searching for other types of work now or in the future, you could perhaps discover what types of opportunities are available in your area.

Malpractice Insurance

You may think that since mental health professionals aren't prescribing medication or performing surgeries that they don't need malpractice insurance. However, it is an important and necessary expense. Unfortunately, we do live in a litigious society. There are various general reasons for clients to file a legal action against you. First, no one is immune to exercising poor judgment – we do make mistakes and missteps. Sometimes those mistakes are indeed missteps and sometimes they are the result of, unfortunately, a lack of competence or a breach of ethics. Further, you may find yourself in a litigious situation because clients, who would obviously be the ones filing lawsuits, are often experiencing high emotional stress, which can cloud their perception. Finally, there are times when people are just not honest and make false accusations.

When you are still in graduate school but begin doing practicum or internship work, your school may require you to purchase student malpractice insurance. If they do not require it, it may still be worth your money. Student insurance is typically inexpensive – rates are usually under $40 per year for a $1,000,000/$3,000,000 policy. It is unlikely that as a student you will be sued, as students are always supervised and your supervisor or university will typically bear the brunt of your liability. Be sure to find this out and then consider that, for less than $50 per year, no matter what the supervisory situation is, it may be worth it to just have your own policy.

Once you are out of school and licensed in your profession, you will want to purchase malpractice insurance. Rates are reasonable and, if you work part time, you may receive a discounted rate. Compared with medical doctors your probability of getting sued is very slim. However, think of it like this. Even if it happens only once in your lifetime your insurance policy will be well worth it. If you work for an agency or a school, you may be covered completely by their policy and have no need for a separate policy. If you are an independent contractor, the practice you work for may insist that you are covered.

You may be wondering why this is so essential. What, specifically, do mental health professionals even get sued for? A defense attorney, who represents mental health professionals such as psychologists and social workers in malpractice cases, writes about some of the most common things that mental health professionals do that leave themselves open to lawsuits or legal action – see Caudill, 2002.

Remember when we discussed boundaries as one of the ethical principles? Several of the pitfalls that Caudill notes concern a blurring of boundaries. For example, he notes that self-disclosure, when it is excessive or inappropriate, can leave a therapist open to legal action. While some self-disclosure may be appropriate if it will help the client, other self-disclosure only occurs because the therapist is still working through his/her own issues with the topic. If a boundary is breached because the therapist enters into a type of relationship, other than client/therapist, this can also leave the therapist open to legal problems. This might involve entering into a business relationship with a client or the even more egregious entering into a sexual relationship with a client. Other things that could lead a client to file legal action against a therapist concern competence issues. Examples of this could include providing therapeutic services that are outside of your area of competence (e.g., doing marriage counseling when you have no training or education in that modality or seeing children when you were not trained for child and adolescent work), not keeping adequate records (or in some cases, unfortunately, keeping no records), or not completing an accurate client history, which could then lead to misdiagnosis or poor treatment planning.

Additionally, Caudill (2002) notes that therapists who diagnose clients with untested, undocumented, and poorly researched "syndromes" such as "malicious mom syndrome" can have legal action leveled against them. This is why the critical thinking skills discussed previously are needed. There will always be new treatments, theories, and ideas. Be careful of jumping on a bandwagon before the treatment or idea can be researched. One of the reasons why clinicians may accept a theory prematurely is because they have not had the scientific or research background to be able to discern those good and bad theories. Don't be one of those clinicians! Be aware of the science that should be expected from those who propose new ideas. Take your research methods classes seriously, because even if you have no desire to conduct research you have a responsibility to evaluate it. This will help your clients and will help keep you out of legal trouble.

Finally, accepting what a client says as truth without using good clinical or critical judgment can cause legal problems. For example, if a mother claims her ex-husband has sexually abused their daughter, you would have a responsibility to carefully question the mother and the child and, hopefully, the father before accepting her claims as valid truth. Contrary to the beliefs of some, people, even children, do lie. Be careful to obtain as much information as you can about a situation before drawing conclusions (yet another critical thinking skill).

As stated earlier, people (both clinicians and clients) can be susceptible to poor judgment and decision-making. Hopefully, your training will help you become adept at these things. However, in case there are lapses or misunderstandings or just out-and-out lies, it is advantageous to protect yourself with malpractice insurance.

Telehealth/Telepsychology/Online Support Groups

I mentioned previously that some psychiatrists are utilizing technology to be able to communicate via the Internet with their patients. The same mechanism is beginning to be used in each of the mental health professions to help counselors/psychologists/social workers engage in therapeutic work with their clients. It is possible to use Skype, online chat services, email, text messaging, or online support groups (especially prominent for substance abuse clients). It can be referred to as telehealth or telepsychology or, by the time you read this, another tele-term. This is still a new modality; however, most professional agencies have begun to compose guidelines that attempt to cover the ethical, legal, and clinical issues related to this. The creators of the following website, http://telehealth.org/ethical-statements/, have compiled a list of all the mental health professions, their guidelines and rules related to using technology to engage in the therapeutic process.

Some of the more salient issues are related to whether the service you provide is covered by traditional malpractice insurance, whether and how conditions of privacy and confidentiality can be effectively maintained, and whether you are practicing within the confines of your own state license if you are interacting with someone in another state. This is a rapidly evolving area, and you can find online guidelines that were written for a particular profession 2 years ago and are already out of date.

I will assume that the issue of e-therapy will be something discussed in your graduate training as the field expands and guidelines are clarified further. I bring it up here because it is an area that you should be aware of when you leave graduate school and begin your own practice. It may not impact you at all, or you may find the concept intriguing. There are even online agencies for which you can work where a client chooses you as their e-therapist and pays a per minute/ per hour fee. When evaluating the usefulness of a novel therapy approach such as this, be sure to exercise your critical thinking skills to ensure that you are working with the primary goal of helping the client.

Prescription Privileges

As you know, only medical doctors (M.D.s) have the authority to prescribe medication. In the mental health field, this means that only psychiatrists can write prescriptions for clients. However, there is a serious shortage of psychiatrists, especially child psychiatrists (Thomas & Holzer, 2006), and psychiatrists who are willing to work with special populations such as prisoners (Fuehrlein, Jha, Brenner, & North, 2011). Back when I was in graduate school in the early 1990s, there was a professor that told our class about a shortage of psychiatrists. So this is not a new phenomenon. He hypothesized that this partially occurs because psychiatry is one of the lowest-paid of the medical specialties. Indeed, *Forbes* magazine (Smith, 2012) lists the highest- and lowest-paying of the medical specialties, and psychiatrists are tied for last place with family practice doctors and pediatric doctors. They each make, on average, about $189,000 per year. Hardly a low salary! However, when you consider that the highest-paid doctors – orthopedic surgeons, cardiologists, and urologists – make $519,000, $512,000, and $461,000, respectively, you may begin to see one reason why medical students are swayed away from psychiatry. Keep in mind that all of these doctors will have to contend with large amounts of student debt and very high malpractice insurance premiums. Add to this the fact that, unlike when you break a leg and can use an X-ray to diagnose the problem, there is no such "X-ray" for most psychiatric disorders, which probably makes it a more difficult area in which to specialize.

This state of affairs is important for all mental health professionals. Most of you, since you are planning to do some form of talk therapy, probably will not (and probably should not) rush to recommending medication. We hope that the training we have will help individuals, couples, and families make changes through insight, behavior modification, altered cognitive distortions, increased social skills, and honed communication skills. However, if you aren't already aware, you will be soon, that there are some psychological issues that will resolve more effectively with medication or with medication combined with talk therapy. For clients who are, for example, seriously depressed or excessively anxious or severely attention deficit-disordered, it is often advantageous to work in conjunction with a doctor to coordinate therapy and medication management. However, there can be up to a six to eight week wait to be seen by a psychiatrist and then several more weeks involved in titrating medication to appropriate levels. Often times, this delay can then also delay the effectiveness of your therapy and counseling.

There are several remedies that the medical community is utilizing to address these issues. First, medical doctors, in general, are experimenting with engaging in telepsychiatry (Smydo, 2014). As discussed earlier, this involves using technology to do psychiatry virtually and reach more people more quickly. Second, I mentioned earlier that we can't X-ray the brain for a diagnosis like we can X-ray an arm or leg. However, significant advances in brain imaging may prove useful for making psychological diagnoses (Sazalavitz, 2013), which may make psychiatry a more desirable field for future doctors. Further, Fuehrlein et al. (2012) propose addressing the shortage of psychiatrists in prisons by encouraging medical schools to give their medical students exposure to that population during their residency training in the hope it might spur their interest. In addition, nurse practitioners are becoming more common in the medical field and they are able to prescribe medication. Nurse practitioners are nurses who have completed advanced training in a medical subspecialty, such as psychiatry. Since they are trained to prescribe medication, another option for a client in need of psychiatric treatment could be to work with a nurse practitioner. Finally, in Unit 1, I discussed primary care psychology, where a mental health practitioner works within a family practice or pediatric office to collaborate with the medical doctor to best serve their patients with mental health concerns. In this way, clients with psychiatric needs can be served in the same office with two collaborating professionals.

Another option that I want to expand upon is one that some psychologists are spearheading. There is a movement underway to allow psychologists to engage in additional training to be qualified to write prescriptions for psychotropic medication and then manage those medications. This push actually began in 1984 when Sen. Daniel Inouye of Hawaii encouraged members of the Hawaii Psychological Association to attempt to earn prescriptive authority. Then, in 1989, the Department of Defense (DoD) was asked by Congress to create what would be called a Psychopharmacology Demonstration Project (PDP) to train clinical psychologists within the military to prescribe medication. In the early and mid-1990s, 10 psychologists completed the program and were then supervised by psychiatrists. The psychiatrists, though initially skeptical, rated the psychologists' quality of care anywhere from good to excellent.

In 2002, New Mexico became the first state to allow psychologists to complete a training program that would allow them prescriptive authority. New Mexico is a very rural state. To illustrate, the National Alliance on Mental Illness (NAMI) (2002) pointed out that, in the early 2000s, New Mexico had 90 licensed psychiatrists; all but 18 lived in either Santa Fe or Albuquerque. This left the rural communities sorely lacking in psychiatric care. New Mexico legislation recognized that there were 400 licensed psychologists, 175 of whom lived outside those two most highly populated areas. Legislators saw them as potential providers of medication and, therefore, granted them prescriptive authority if they engaged in additional psychopharmacology training.

Since New Mexico granted prescription rights to psychologists, two more states have followed suit. Psychologists who have taken advanced training in psychopharmacology and have been supervised in prescribed clinical settings (APA, 2014) are eligible to prescribe medication in Louisiana (2004) and Illinois (2014). There are some limitations to their privileges, such as those in Illinois cannot prescribe for children, elderly, or pregnant women. However, this is still a significant step forward for psychologists and clients in need. It will also be of use to other mental health professionals who struggle to find appropriate psychiatric care for their more troubled clients.

Note that there are many who opposed this initiative, including many psychologists. Those psychologists passionate about their dissent on the issue have even created Psychologists Opposed to Prescription Privileges for Psychologists (POPPP). Most significantly, members of POPPP and the American Medical Association (AMA) are adamant that psychologists could not get enough training to prescribe responsibly without completing medical school. Specifically, it is thought that psychologists do not have the basic foundational training to learn the psychopharmacology necessary to be a prescriber. For example, the background training of psychologists does not include courses in biology and chemistry. Critics feel that taking a short training program without that basic science foundation will set psychologists up to do a less-than-satisfactory job prescribing. NAMI (2002) noted two other reasons why some may be opposed to prescription authority for psychologists. The first is that psychologists are trained more in social and behavioral approaches than they are in the medical model and that this does not lend itself to providing medical treatment appropriately. Psychologists, however, counter that they do indeed consider biological influences on individuals and on individuals' behavior and that most psychologists espouse a biopsychosocial model of treatment. Second, NAMI (2002) reports that those opposed to prescription privileges for psychologists point out that over 50% of people being prescribed a psychotropic medication are also being treated for other serious medical issues that a psychologist would not be trained in or competent to treat.

Be aware of this issue as you embark on your graduate studies and, later on, the practice of your discipline. Given that the movement for prescription privileges has now netted three states that have granted authority to psychologists is an indication that the issue will not go away. However, you could also perceive that this fight began in 1984 and has gained footing in only three states thus far. So perhaps there is not much progress. Notwithstanding whether you agree or disagree with the idea of psychologists receiving privileges, you should be aware of the national issue of there being a shortage of medical professionals, namely psychiatrists, who specialize in mental health and the biochemical treatment of it. The debate is worth following if it will help ensure that the underserved areas of the country receive psychiatric treatment, whether that is through psychologists who receive privileges or through the medical community continuing to expand ways that they offer psychiatric services.

References

American Psychological Association (2014, June 25). APA applauds landmark Illinois law allowing psychologists to prescribe medications. Retrieved from http://www.apa.org/news/press/releases/2014/06/prescribe-medications. aspx.

Caudill, B. (2002). Malpractice and licensing pitfalls for therapists: A defense attorney's list. In L. VandeCreek & T. L. Jackson (Eds.), *Innovations in clinical practice: A source book* (vol. 20). Sarasota, FL: Professional Resource Press.

Fuehrlein, B. S., Jha, M. K., Brenner, A. M., & North, C. S. (2012). Can we address the shortage of psychiatrists in the correctional setting with exposure during residency training? *North Community Mental Health Journal,* 48(6), 756–760.

NAMI (2002). Prescribing privileges for psychologists: An overview. Retrieved from https://www2.nami.org/Template.cfm?Section=Issue_ Spotlights&template=/ContentManagement/ContentDisplay. cfm&ContentID=8375.

Sazalavitz, M. (2013). Talk therapy or antidepressant: A brain scan predicts which works best for your depression. Retrieved from http://healthland. time.com/2013/06/17/talk-therapy-or-antidepressant-a-brain-scan-predicts-which-works-best-for-your-depression/.

Smith, J. (2012, July 20). The best and worst paying jobs for doctors. *Forbes.* Retrieved from http://www.forbes.com/sites/jacquelynsmith/2012/ 07/20/the-best-and-worst-paying-jobs-for-doctors-2/2/.

Smydo, J. (2014, March 16). Psychiatrists in short supply nationwide: Lower pay, limited respect for specialty blamed for scarcity. *Pittsburgh Post Gazette.* Retrieved from http://www.post-gazette.com/news/health/ 2014/03/16/Psychiatrists-in-short-supply-nationwide-Pittsburgh/ stories/201403160076.

Thomas, C. R., & Holzer, C. E. (2006). The continuing shortage of child and adolescent psychiatrists. *Journal of the American Academy of Child and Adolescent Psychiatry,* 45(9), 1023–1031.

Conclusion

We have come to the end of our discussion of careers and mental health career-related issues. But before we finish, I want to commend you on even considering a career in the area of mental health. The types of skills you will learn throughout your studies, should you choose to proceed with this career choice, are very necessary in our society today. Statistics found on the National Alliance on Mental Illness (NAMI) website (https://www.nami.org/Learn-More/Mental-Health-By-the-Numbers) give a snapshot of the severity of the problem of mental illness in our country. In a given year, NAMI notes that 1 in 5 adults (43.7 million people) will suffer from a diagnosable mental illness. About 1 in 25 (13.6 million people) will experience a serious mental illness that substantially impairs or limits his or her lifestyle. Further, 1 in 5 adolescents between the ages of 12 and 18 lives with a mental illness; the most common problems are mood disorders, behavior disorders (e.g., conduct disorder), and anxiety disorders.

In addition to these general numbers, NAMI reports that the rates of mental illness are even higher in certain special populations. For example, almost 1 in 4 individuals living in homeless shelters struggles with mental illness. If you consider mental illness AND substance abuse, that number jumps from 1 in 4 to 1 in 2. Further, 1 in 5 adult prisoners have a mental illness, but, more significantly, almost 3 in 4 youths in juvenile prisons have a mental health condition. All these numbers are

Careers in Mental Health: Opportunities in Psychology, Counseling, and Social Work, First Edition. Kim Metz.
© 2016 John Wiley & Sons, Ltd. Published 2016 by John Wiley & Sons, Ltd.

meant to illustrate how significant a problem mental illness is in our society. The field needs enthusiastic and well-trained individuals to help treat mental illness, so please realize that your potential contributions will be very welcomed! In your career search, be aware of the dire need for help for special populations, such as the homeless and prisoners. These are underserved populations who may be able to thrive if their underlying mental health issue could be addressed properly.

In summary, we have explored the nuts and bolts of the various mental health professions and have discussed general issues related to doing mental health work. I hope that the information in this text has helped you in your search for your career. As I stated in the Introduction, you will have your career for many years and will spend many hours a week engaged in it. It should be something you enjoy, and you should enter into it fully informed. Just the fact that you have read this text all the way through indicates that you are likely to choose one of these mental health professions as your career. I wish you the best in your pursuit!

Index

AA *see* Alcoholics Anonymous
AACD *see* American Association
    for Counseling and
    Development
AAMC *see* American Association for
    Marriage Counseling
AAMFT *see* American Association
    of Marriage and Family
    Therapists
AAMFT Code of Ethics, 137
addiction counseling, 64, 79–80, 85
Alcoholics Anonymous, 80–81
alcoholism, concept of, in 1956,
    80–81, 83
AMA *see* American Medical
    Association
American Association for Counseling
    and Development, 61
American Association for Marriage
    Counseling, 73
American Association of Marriage
    and Family Therapists, 69, 74
American Counseling Association,
    58, 137

American Counseling Association
    Code of Ethics, 137
American Medical Association,
    81, 165
American Mental Health Counselors
    Association, 60
American Personnel and Guidance
    Association, 59, 61
American Psychological Association,
    3–4, 9–12, 15, 22, 30–34,
    59, 61, 92, 94, 97, 101, 137,
    142–143, 152, 164
American School Counselor
    Association, 59, 99
American Social Worker Board, 49
AMFTRB *see* Association of Marital
    and Family Therapy
    Regulatory Boards
    Examination
AMHCA *see* American Mental
    Health Counselors
    Association
APA *see* American Psychological
    Association

Careers in Mental Health: Opportunities in Psychology, Counseling, and Social Work,
First Edition. Kim Metz.
© 2016 John Wiley & Sons, Ltd. Published 2016 by John Wiley & Sons, Ltd.